Listening to the Animals

ANIMAL WISDOM

EDITED BY PHYLLIS HOBE

A GUIDEPOSTS BOOK

ACKNOWLEDGMENTS

Every attempt has been made to credit the sources of copyrighted material used in this book. If any such acknowledgment has been inadvertently omitted or miscredited, receipt of such information would be appreciated.

All material that originally appeared in *Guideposts* magazine, *Angels on Earth* or *Daily Guideposts* is reprinted with permission. Copyright © 1973, 1994, 1996.

"Ask and You Will Receive," by Christie Craig, is used by permission of the author.

"Susie," by Tom Maveety, appeared in *Dog & Kennel,* April 2000.

"Lessons Along a Country Road," by Diane Komp, appeared in *Daily Guideposts 1994.*

"Buster" is from *Dogs With Jobs,* by Merrily Weisbord and Kim Kachanoff, D.V.M. Copyright © 2000 by Kim Kachanoff and Merrily Weisbord. Published by Pocket Books, a division of Simon & Schuster, Inc.

"Rosie, the Lifesaver," by Julia Glass, appeared in *Redbook,* January 1995.

"Whose Birds Are These?" is from *The Swan in My Bathtub,* by Mary Jane Stretch and Phyllis Hobe. Copyright © Mary Jane Stretch and Merit Books, Inc., 1991. Published by Dutton, a division of Penguin Books USA Inc.

"Good Morning," by Shari Smyth, appeared in *Daily Guideposts 1996.*

"Rio's Journey" and "An Angel Named Taffy," by Anne Watkins, are used by permission of the author.

"Battle Tactics" is from *The Dog Who Wouldn't Be,* by Farley Mowat; copyright © 1957 by the Curtis Publishing Company; © copyright 1957 by Farley Mowat.

"A Dog-Gone Case" and "Sharing the Pain," by Nancy B. Gibbs, are used by permission of the author.

"Persisto, the Squirrel," by Karen King Murphy, is used by permission of the author.

"A Memorable Battle," by Fred Bauer, appeared in *Daily Guideposts 1996.*

"How Kato Was Rescued," by Graham Phalen, is from *Circles of Compassion,* edited by Elaine Sichel. Text copyright © 1995, 1998 Elaine Sichel. Published by Voice & Vision Publishing.

"Places of the Heart," by Taimur Mahmood, appeared in *DOGworld,* January 2000.

"The Bird Feeder," by Scott Walker, appeared in *Daily Guideposts 1996.*

"A Little Kitten From Nowhere," by Sissy Burggraf, is used by permission of the author.

"Oliver's Shadow," by Lillian Roberts, is used by permission of the author.

"Merry's Look Into the Future," by Herb Kugel, appeared in *Dog & Kennel,* April 2000.

"Out of the Nest," by Kathryn Lay, is used by permission of the author.

(continued on page 208)

Designed by SMS Typography
Illustrations by Ron Bucalo
Jacket designed by Dennis Arnold
Printed in the United States of America

Contents

OVERCOMING OBSTACLES

IN TOUCH WITH GOD

LESSONS IN LIVING

Always Understanding

Introduction

I used to think that I was the one who taught my animals how to live in our world. Actually, it was the other way around. While I was busy teaching them how to Sit, Stay, Come and Heel, plus a few lovable tricks such as Speak, Roll Over and Shake Hands, they, in their quiet way, were teaching me about more important things, such as kindness, patience, loyalty, love and even good judgment. Finally I caught on: they were my teachers. They know far more about living in our world than I ever will, so it's not at all surprising that God often uses his animals to bring us the guidance we need.

In ANIMAL WISDOM, one of the books in Guideposts' exclusive series, *LISTENING TO THE ANIMALS,* we offer our thanks for the many lessons we learn from the animals in our lives. These true stories demonstrate how they bring us closer to God and help us to become better human beings.

The animals in *Everyday Blessings,* our first chapter, awaken us to the beauty of our daily lives. In "Whose Birds Are These?" Mary Jane Stretch, a wildlife rehabilitator, relishes the opportunity to help a mother bird raise her young and is rewarded with a farewell visit. Buster, an Australian cattle dog, brings companionship and a sense of purpose to a biking cowboy during a day of challenging work. In "Rio's Journey," Anne

Watkins tells us about a sick parrot who charmed her into taking him home.

In *Overcoming Obstacles* we meet some remarkable animals who solve their problems with courage and intelligence. Mutt, Farley Mowat's childhood dog, has to figure out how to outwit some neighborhood bullies, and does it with style. Karen King Murphy learns the meaning of determination from Persisto, a backyard squirrel who outwits every attempt to keep him from a bird feeder. In "How Kato Was Rescued," Graham Phalen describes the dramatic attempts to help a horse trapped in a mountain crevice.

In Touch With God brings us stories about the deeply spiritual nature of animals. Taimur Mahmood's "Places of the Heart" is a touching account of a man and his animal friends as they explore some of the most beautiful parts of the natural world. "A Little Kitten From Nowhere," by Sissy Burggraf, is about the extraordinary friendship between a young cat and an elderly dog who is losing his sight and hearing. And Susan Chernak McElroy introduces us to a llama we will never forget.

The memorable animals in *Lessons in Living* seem to be in the right place at the right time when people need their encouragement and example. Clare, a disabled but gallant chicken, teaches Jan Rogers about the value of life and hope. In "Wild Kingdom," Kethry, Paula Wilshe's cat, proves herself to be a devoted mother, even though she almost wrecks the family home while doing it. "One," Gene Hill's sensitive story about a man and his dog, will stay with you long after you read it.

In *Always Understanding*, we meet Lowell, Gay Balliet's delightful pig, and as we discover his extraordinary intelligence and affection, we can't help wishing he were ours. Anne Stockton's short, insightful tribute to her cat, Honey-Bun, puts into words the deep feelings we all have for a beloved pet. We also follow Props, a really smart pup, as he makes the rounds of the sets in the movie studio where he earns his living as an actor.

The wonderful creatures in ANIMAL WISDOM remind us of the animals in our own lives, and we remember the many times they have nurtured our spirits and helped us to solve our problems. There is no mystery about the source of their courage, dedication, unselfishness and compassion: the source is God.

PHYLLIS HOBE

ANIMAL
WISDOM

Everyday Blessings

"I don't think I could live without an animal in my life."

ANNEMARIE LUCAS

$\mathcal{H}$ave you ever noticed animals sitting still for a long time, enjoying the scenery? Take a few minutes out of your busy day and join them. You'll begin to see the world as you've never seen it before if you look at it through their eyes. They know what matters.

When you come home to your animals, they make you feel important. They let you know they love you. You matter.

Go ahead. Follow their example. It will change your life.

Ask and You Will Receive

CHRISTIE CRAIG

$\mathcal{M}$y husband had just been laid off from his job, my grandmother had just passed away, and my daughter hated her new teacher. There seemed to be nothing good or positive in my life. Having always been optimistic, I didn't know how to deal with this sense of gloom that hung on for almost a month. Someone had recommended I start reading daily devotionals. The theme for the week was: Ask and you will receive.

Feeling too down to draw comfort from the words of wisdom, I abandoned the book on the coffee table and went about my daily schedule. One of my many chores was to cut and groom my Lhasa Apso, Muffie. Most grooming days, I enjoyed the one-on-one time with my pet, but lately nothing intrigued me.

As we sat on the back porch, cutting, clipping and still grimacing, I suddenly felt the first drop of rain. Sensing my mood grow darker along with the sky, I hurried with the job and ran inside, leaving the mess of dog hair strewn over my patio. Once inside I went to the window to see the wind stirring the hair about. "Great," I mumbled. "Now I have even a bigger mess to clean up. Can't You give me a break?" I snapped to the ceiling in a hurried prayer and closed my eyes in frustration.

Not long after that, my normally calm Muffie began to bark. I found her at the bay window facing the back patio. The first thing I noticed was that the sun had returned and the wind had blown the clouds away. The second thing I noticed was the swarm of sparrows. Chirping and jumping about, the tiny brown-and-tan birds were filling their beaks with blond dog hair, then flying to the trees to line their nests with their great find.

Immediately, I glanced over to my devotional book, still open on the coffee table. I remembered the theme, Ask and you will receive, and I recalled my poorly spoken prayer for help. Laughing and crying at the same time, I leaned against the wall, slid down, and sat on the floor. Muffie climbed into my lap, licked away a few of my tears, and together we watched as the birds took away the "mess" I hadn't wanted to clean up.

I sat there for the next hour, giving and being given affection by Muffie—just the break I'd needed, and had requested. Between the unconditional love of a pet and the message that God would be with me even in my darkest days, my mood, like the day, suddenly brightened.

Susie

TOM MAVEETY

I had just finished my shower one spring afternoon when I heard the sounds of crying outside. I quickly dressed and headed for the front door. She had traveled in the trunk of my uncle's car from a small farm in Indiana. The trip had made the tiny beagle puppy anxious. As my uncle held her in his arms, she finally turned toward me. When her beautiful brown eyes met mine, I instantly fell in love.

Her name came to me shortly after my uncle left—Susie. There was no barking yet because of her age, but her small cries and fear quickly faded as she became more comfortable.

My mother and I made a small bed for her in the corner of the living room. During those first weeks, she would often go to sleep in unusual positions that struck us with laughter. Her chewing, however, was not a laughing matter. We got Susie on a Saturday. By Monday morning, we'd blocked off the entire kitchen with dining room furniture so that Susie's constant chewing could not inflict further damage upon the rest of the house.

Susie would reside in her fortress until we came home. One morning I returned from my class to find Susie had disappeared from the kitchen. I looked through the entire house in a frantic state, wondering where she had gone, until I finally came to my bedroom. Yawning and with just a hint of sleepiness in her eyes, Susie walked out from behind my closet doors, wagging her tail. Laughing, I took her in my arms, amazed that she somehow found her way out of the maze we created.

Susie also found her way out of our fenced back yard several times to investigate the field behind our home. The trees there were just too inviting for a creature born to smell. A neighbor told us that he noticed her by the trees a short distance from our house and returned her to our yard. My legs felt like rubber, realizing Susie could've easily gotten lost.

It wasn't long before Susie negotiated her way onto our beds at night. My mother's was always her favorite, because it provided more room. Some nights she would sleep with me, however, and I would try to hold her warm body next to mine for as long as possible. Soon her cold, moist nose would dip into my ear, and the loud sounds of breathing would prohibit me from sleep. It wouldn't be long before she would have her fill of me as well, stretching her legs and making her way back to Mom's more spacious accommodations.

As she got older, Susie began to settle down. No longer was there a constant urge for attention. She was content to just be with us and take an occasional walk around the neighborhood. Her favorite outing was our daily trip through a nearby, squirrel-filled park each morning after we dropped Mom off at work. Susie's back hair would rise and her body shook violently as she anticipated her daily encounter with her mortal adversary. Once she was so excited she climbed through a partially open car window. As she darted away from the moving car in pursuit of the squirrel, she left a zigzagging trail of leaves flying in the autumn breeze. I stopped the car and began my chase on foot, fearing a car would hit her. I could see her eyes looking back at me in an attempt to explain her behavior. It was clear there was a conflict between knowing she was misbehaving and obeying her instincts. Finally she slipped, giving me just enough time to catch her. Knowing she had upset me, Susie licked my face over and over, wagging her tail, panting happily.

Susie was always a comforting source of companionship. When I was sad, she was there to console me with soft licks and a wagging tail that assured me of her love. In return I almost always let her have her way.

Through the years she stopped chasing balls and wrestling with me when I came home from work. Her gray snout and white hairs told me she was a lady now, getting on in years. In August last year Susie took a sharp turn as she made her way out the door and into the yard to bark at a squirrel invading her territory, and in doing so detached her hind leg at the joint.

Her limping seemed to get better, then worse. After several trips to the vet, Susie was put into a cast. The constant limping somehow dislocated her shoulder area. There was no noticeable improvement for days, then weeks. Susie was often sedated and unable to move.

One evening Mom called me at work. In a frantic voice she told me Susie was in deep trouble. There was simply no relief anywhere for Susie, Mom explained. With her head sunk low, unable to raise it without pain, Susie traveled from room to room, seeking comfort that could not be found. When I got the news, I knew that I had to show the ultimate act of love. My dog was hurting.

I was married now. I called my wife and asked her to meet Mom and I at the pet emergency center a short distance from where I worked. Susie was in much more pain than when I had left her earlier that day. I loved her so much, but I knew I had to accept the fact it was time to let her go. I remembered telling her so often, "If I could only get inside your head and tell you how much you mean to me." Now, kissing her between the eyes, I told it to her for the last time.

My emotions overcame me and I became a sobbing thirty-four-year-old. Susie lay in a pink blanket, her eyes were slightly open, and I could see her tongue, the tongue that licked away so many of my tears. She lay quietly in painless peace, as I stroked her soft head for the final time. I will miss her; I love her so much. I always will.

from DOG & KENNEL

Lessons Along a Country Road

DIANE KOMP

If you lived near me, you could learn a lot about tending God's creation. To get to my country home, I have to drive along a winding road lined with exotic plantings and inhabited by strange animals.

One of my neighbors spent the whole summer cultivating his garden and planting a new border of witches'-broom shrubs for all of us to enjoy. The first weekend, one of his new shrubs disappeared. A little farther down the road lives a new "neighbor"—a wild turkey who has moved into our woods. On a pleasant day, she thinks nothing of sitting down in the center of the road to enjoy a midday sunbath. The first time I saw her, I was driving a bit faster than usual and nearly ran her down. Within one block, two endangered species!

But I don't see the situation as hopeless. The gardener replaced the shrub and planted a large, clearly worded sign: SHAME ON YOU. Six weeks have passed and his garden—our garden—remains inviolate. And our turkey-lady is still out there strutting and sunning. She has not changed her ways at all, but I have changed mine. I'm careful to obey the posted speed limit on our country road.

I think about the missing witches'-broom and the predictably unpredictable turkey, and I realize that there is hope for all endangered species if each of us will do our part. I can start on my own country road. Reverence and respect for nature is a lesson that is best taught one plant and one wild turkey at a time.

Buster

MERRILY WEISBORD AND KIM KACHANOFF, D.V.M.

Buster's forehead crinkles as he stares hard into the ferns and scrub surrounding the peppermint tree. An old cow lies straining on her side. She shudders, her four legs rising off the ground in a great effort to rid herself of some unseen burden. Buster watches anxiously as she bellows out her pain.

With Buster's attention distracted by the suffering cow, the other cattle stream around the tree, across the gully, and onto the other side of the creek. Buster hears Gary's trail bike buzzing up and down the far bank, trying to collect the errant cows and calves into one tight group. Still, Buster doesn't leave the laboring female. He edges forward and sniffs her hindquarters. Spotting a tiny protruding wet leg, Buster knows it's time to get help.

He takes off at a lope, but doesn't follow the creek like an inexperienced jackeroo on his first cattle drive. Instead, he seeks out the high ground running along the ridge to an old road he knows from chasing kangaroos, his favorite recreation. Silhouetted against the gray, overcast sky, Buster's strides eat up the ground. Within minutes, he spots the main herd below. Gary is charging back and forth like an angry bull as Taco, the rookie "doggeroo," struggles to help control the herd.

Buster heads off Gary's dusty bike, running alongside, then

leading him back toward the creek and the stricken cow. Gary has no choice but to follow—he can't herd the cattle without Buster, and, besides, "Buster's my best mate, why would he lead me wrong?" Standing on the pedals to absorb the pounding shock, Gary follows his streaking Australian cattle dog across the rolling Queensland prairies.

At the top of the ridge, Buster disappears. Gary slams on the brakes and slides to a stop. Buster reemerges from the bushes, trots over to the bike, and lies down, looking at Gary as if to say, "I did my job, partner, now you do yours."

Parting the leafy tree fronds, Gary sees the birthing cow.

Buster's decision to suspend cattle driving and come to the aid of the endangered cow was guided by the complex mix of genes that constitute the Australian cattle dog. Ranchers developed this hardworking breed to move cattle efficiently across the wide open spaces of Australia's interior, where fences are scarce and ranch hands even scarcer.

Australian cattle dogs trace their roots back to the 1830s and a breed called the Smithfield, a sheepdog imported to Australia from England. The Smithfield had incredible stamina and could run all day, but its frequent barking caused the cattle to bolt and stampede. To overcome this drawback, an enterprising cattleman crossed the Smithfield with a hunting canine that never barked, the Australian wild dog, or dingo. The resulting dog controlled cattle silently by biting their hind legs, but was itself completely uncontrollable.

Ranchers then tried to mitigate the wildness of these "biters" by cross-breeding them with the smooth-coated Highland collie, a Scottish working dog with a distinctly colored blue merle coat. This mix produced an obedient dog that bit cattle on the heel on command. Unfortunately, the barking problem was back again. A third crossbreeding attempt added another dash of dingo, doubling the dingo dose to create the dog known as a Heeler. Heelers proved popular, but wreaked havoc during the cattle drives to market by insisting on herding the horses as well. Finally, two ingenious ranching brothers solved the conundrum by introducing dalmatian bloodlines, a breed known for its compatibility with horses and its work with horse-drawn fire wagons. The resulting offspring was then crossed with the kelpie, an Australian version of the Border collie. The final version of the Australian cattle dog was a red-speckled dog like Buster (or, in other cases, blue), half dingo, half combination of the other breeds. This canine composite possesses a reliable temperament and independent reasoning. Alert, quiet, strong, and tireless, the breed was accepted into the Australian Kennel Club in 1903.

Buster opens one eye just before dawn. From the front porch, he sees the Southern Cross shining brilliantly above the horizon and pink fingers reaching up into the eastern sky. His ears tilt forward and through the screen door he hears the sizzle of two eggs plopping into a pan. The aroma of bacon curls around his nose.

Buster glances alertly toward the paddock. The fenced-in enclosure is empty, willowy peppermint trees waiting silently to shelter the shade-seeking Angus and Murray Grey cattle that will be brought home at the end of the day by seven-year-old Buster and his human companion, Gary. For three years, it's been just the two of them, with an occasional new pup, like the sixteen-month-old female, Taco, to train.

Buster knows the routine well. A big breakfast of bacon and eggs means a long, hard day driving cattle.

"Here, boy." The screen door swings open. "Did ya have a good night?"

Forty-two-year-old Gary Bazely places breakfast in front of Buster, scratches him between the ears, and unhooks his chain. Buster snaps up the small piece of steak that sits as a special treat on top of the dry food, and wags his tail hard, moist nose knocking bits of kibble onto the ground. He licks it all up and leaps down off the porch to join Gary. Before the tall, rangy cattleman can adjust his helmet and kick-start his trail bike, Buster has reached the creek, Taco close behind. They lap up the fresh flowing water, eyes glued to Gary.

The biking cowboy kicks his mechanical steed into gear and the two dogs explode out of the creek, spraying geysers of water. Forelegs fully extended, neck bobbing, and hind legs reaching ahead for maximum power, Buster runs beside Gary across the Australian plain. Taco slows to a trot, still developing her stamina, too young yet to maintain the ground-eating pace. Gary and Buster, cowboy and cowdog, speed over rolling hills through glens of flowering bramble, Buster agilely leaping the small water courses, Gary picking his way across the rocky bottomed, flowing streams. Together, they head to Gary's farthest pastureland, the "outback" of his 1,060-acre ranch.

An hour later, Buster and Gary reach their destination. From a hilltop overlooking the grazing field, they survey sixty of Gary's finest cows and calves—breeding stock and beef cattle ready for auction.

"Let's git 'em moving," Gary says. Buster needs no more encouragement. He heads off down a small coulee, staying hidden until he is on the far side of the cattle, trots right to pull in the herd, back left to tighten the flank, and moves in expertly from behind to push them forward. More than a hundred and fifty years of inventive selective breeding has created the perfect cowpoke on four legs. Gary watches his partner at work, always amazed that a dog with no formal training knows instinctively from an early age exactly what has to be done.

"One year old is a little late to break in a cattle dog," Kathe, a top breeder of Australian cattle dogs, told him, "but Buster is a good one." As a pup, Buster passed the broom test like a good heeler. "A good Australian cattle dog isn't scared of a charging eight-hundred-pound bull, so a broom's not going to faze them, even as a pup," Kathe explained. "Buster didn't only heel the broom, he also herded and nipped the seven other pups in his litter."

Gary took to the yearling from the moment he arrived, and the two quickly became great mates. To train him, all Gary had to do was be patient. Buster was a natural and caught on quickly.

Buster sweeps wide through the grass, stopping now and then to check the cows. Gary follows him down the hill, keeping his distance, holding back the newly arrived, panting Taco. Gary can see the dingo in Buster—the triangular, permanently erect ears, short muscular neck, bushy tail, and the stealth of his wild ancestors. Buster moves silently behind the cows. He stops, lowers his head slightly, and "eyes" three large dark Angus and a lighter Murray Grey. Responding to the glare of this tough little dog with its sharp teeth, the cows move briskly toward the cow path at the end of the pasture.

But two younger cows and a calf aren't yet ready to leave the dew-damp grass of the valley. They move languidly in the wrong direction, toward a brook at the pasture's edge.

"Go git 'em," Gary orders.

Wheeling about, Buster gallops to the right of the cows, his reddish coat blending into the brown grass along the side of the forest. He darts behind the largest straggler, crouches low, and with impeccable timing bites her right rear leg just as she steps down on it. Hopping onto her left leg, the cow lashes out with the right. But in the split second of her half step, Buster drops flat to the ground, and the cow's thrust cuts harmlessly through the air.

"He took a few to the head before learning cows are smarter than brooms," Gary remembers, thinking how keen his dog was, how quickly he caught on.

One more nip and the rogue cow trots to rejoin the herd. Buster takes a few steps toward the remaining two, and they quickly follow suit.

"Come behind," Gary calls, and Buster returns to the bike. Taco has succeeded in rounding up a few stragglers and the herd progresses up and over the hill. Now Gary works the lead, staying a little off to the side with Taco until they reach a shallow stream. Here, the herd splits, half fording the stream, half following the trail on Gary's side of the embankment.

"Git 'em, git 'em," Gary calls to Buster. "Git 'em NOW," he yells more urgently, knowing that upstream the water will be too deep to cross and collecting the herd again will be tough.

Buster has anticipated the danger. He moves quickly in a wide loop, coming around from downstream and cutting off the oncoming cows. He stops short to give them ample space to turn around, then rushes in with a few fake lunges. The cows splash back across the shallow part of the stream. Gary is ahead, out of sight with the first group, so Buster works the breakaway cattle from behind. When they stop to munch grass, he stops too. Only when they deviate from the path home does he move in and turn them, nipping and ducking to the ground when gentler methods fail. He catches up to Gary at a small pond. His thirty head join Gary's and the sixty cattle drink their fill.

"Go, boy, go, girl," Gary says encouragingly. Without hesitation, his two dusty dogs wade happily among the cattle for watery relief.

The sun arcs high in the sky, signaling the temperature has climbed to over a hundred degrees.

"Git 'em up, put 'em up," Gary urges, aware of the paucity of shade between the pond and the paddock. The dogs fan out to either side of the pond. Buster shows "eye," body flexed and ready to dash in if his authority is challenged. The cattle begin to move out, the whole herd soon back in motion. Gary is on his bike, Taco close by, Buster in the rear, moving the stragglers. Moving cattle is a two- to three-man job, but in ranch country outside Kingaroy, hands are scarce.

"Don't know what I'd do without Buster," Gary smiles to himself, watching his dog on the far side of the creek bringing in the last of the cattle. "He works harder than two hands and eats a lot less."

Gary turns the lead cows down the side path toward the ranch, Taco on guard at the fork. Despite her valiant efforts, half the cows forge straight ahead into the green grass beyond.

"Git 'em, git 'em," Gary calls to Buster.

But Buster is nowhere to be seen.

Gary speeds off to forestall the wandering cattle, leaving Taco to do the best she can at the turn.

"It's unlike Buster to abandon his post," Gary worries, feeling the strangeness of being on the plains without his dog. Buster is always with him—whether trotting along on the drive, lying close by at night, sitting by the bike, guarding the "ute," or utility truck, chasing the departing vehicle until it moves out of sight, or waiting on the porch of the farmhouse until he spies the telltale dust of Gary's return. All this flashes through Gary's mind as he scours the horizon for Buster and scrambles to collect the rapidly disappearing herd.

Buster reappears, running hard, without thought for the cattle spread out like water from a broken dam. Angling his body beside the dirt bike, he cuts Gary off, then leads him urgently along the beaten "'roo" track used by kangaroos. Overhanging ferns slap the cattleman's helmet, but the route brings them quickly to the stricken cow. Rolling up his sleeves, Gary gets down on his knees and braces himself, one hand on the cow's rump, the other firmly grasping the calf's slippery protruding hind leg. It's a breech birth and the calf is dangerously positioned, one hind leg trapped inside. If Gary doesn't get it out soon, the calf will die from lack of oxygen. Gary pushes the little leg back into the cow's pelvic opening to give himself room to maneuver, and rotates the calf into position with a half twist. Close behind, Buster watches his master grasp both the calf's hind legs, and pull gently in time to the laboring cow's contractions. Two minutes later, the sticky, wet newborn slides out onto the ground. Gary quickly clears the mucus plugs from its small nostrils and vigorously rubs its sides to stimulate its breathing. Excited, Buster noses his way in and gives the bleating calf a helpful nudge. Taking Buster's hint, the exhausted mother cow struggles to her feet and begins licking and cleaning her baby.

"Atta boy, Buster!" Buster's tail thumps happily. "Good

boy." Gary knows that without Buster both cow and calf would be dead. He grabs his dog around the neck, shaking his big, broad head. Buster licks his master's face. Gary looks back toward the bush, then to Buster, who has once more fulfilled his breed standard's promise of a dog that is "courageous and trustworthy, with an implicit devotion to duty."

"Let's go git 'em," he says, and Buster is off. The herd's stolen pasture holiday comes to an abrupt end. It's late afternoon, the clouds have broken up, and the cattle are back on the dirt track home. The sun is sinking behind the tall green mountains of the Great Dividing Range, shooting golden spires into the sky. Buster, Gary, and Taco spot the farmhouse on the rise.

"Put 'em up," Gary calls, and Buster quickens his pace. Gary speeds ahead and opens the gate, waving his hat at the cows as they flood into the paddock. Buster pushes the last one in. "He hates stragglers," Gary thinks, and closes the gate.

Gary beats the dust off his pants as he walks beside Buster up to the house. He can almost taste the cold Foster's, almost smell the steak on the barbie. This is his favorite time of the day and Buster's, too, but not for relaxing. The cattle driving over, Buster wants some good ol' cowpoke fun. Gary's hand reaches out to scratch Buster's head, but touches air. He turns to see Buster, a dusty ball shooting toward the pasture, where six silvery kangaroos are enjoying an evening nibble. The dog slices through the middle of the pack and shoots out the other side, turning and simultaneously trying to pick up speed. He heads for one kangaroo, veers off to another, pushing half the 'roos into the shelter of the trees, the other half left milling in the field. Gary laughs, seeing his dog torn between his two ancestral instincts: herding and chasing. In a last sprint, Buster chases the remaining 'roos into the woods, turns, and trots contentedly toward home, finally ready to call it a full wrangling day.

from DOGS WITH JOBS

Rosie, the Lifesaver

JULIA GLASS

"When my husband is on the road doing computer consulting, Rosie and I are inseparable," says Cheryl Essex, 40, of Garden City Beach, South Carolina. Her companion, Rosie O'Grady, a 6-year-old schnauzer-Westie, has a mellow disposition, a "charming" personality, and—as Cheryl discovered one evening a year and a half ago—a nose tuned to trouble.

Cheryl, a property manager, was on the phone when Rosie started yelping and darting to and from the front door. Alarmed, Cheryl opened it and immediately smelled gasoline. After phoning 911, she alerted neighbors in her apartment building to evacuate. Firemen soon discovered towels soaked in gasoline planted in the building's stairwells—the interrupted handiwork of an arsonist. No arrest was ever made, though Rosie was the toast of the community for months.

Recently, the Essexes moved to a new home. "One of the first things we're doing is installing a chain ladder as an extra precaution. But for Rosie, I've got a basket tied to a rope," says Cheryl. "If ever there is a fire, she'll go down first, *then* us."

from REDBOOK

"Whose Birds Are These?"

MARY JANE STRETCH

The fledgling tree is a big old pine that grows right alongside the house where I live and work. I can't imagine how any tree could grow to suit my needs so perfectly, but somehow this one did—and long before I came here. When I moved into the house during the seventies, the shrubs and other trees had grown over the windows on both floors and all the way up to the roof. Little by little my daughters and I cut them back to let some light into the house, and one day we hacked our way through to the tree.

I had known that an evergreen was back there. I could see its needles poking through the jungle in front of it. But *such* a tree! I stepped back in admiration. "It's a fledgling tree!" I said to the girls. "This is where we'll put the baby birds when they're ready to fly."

My daughters were not impressed. It was hot, and they had better things to do. Besides, there was always that little irritation whenever I turned my attention to my wild offspring. Like all children, mine did not want to share their mother. They did not, and still do not, know quite how to deal with the thousands of animals and birds who have rightfully claimed me as a mother of sorts. I do not agree with my daughters when they say that my work deprives them of me; they have always come first, and I think they know that. But when you're a wildlife rehabilitator, you don't work regular hours and then quit. The need is always there, and you do what has to be done.

"Okay, we'll knock off for now," I said, and immediately Debbie and Leah disappeared around the side of the house. They were fourteen and ten at the time, quite independent. But Sammy was only six, and was too young to tag along with her sisters or go off on her own. Since she did not like being restricted, I tried to interest her in the tree.

"See, Sammy," I said, running my hand along the thick branch that grew downward at a steep angle from the main trunk and then leveled off for a few feet before it turned upward again. "This is just right for the baby birds. It's only about three feet off the ground, so they can fly up here easily. Then they can sit on the branch until they're ready to go higher or back down." The level part of the branch was bare of needles and looked like a mighty brown bicep, a good four inches across. A fledgling would feel secure there. And at the very end of the branch, where it turned upward again, was thick foliage. A bird could hide there.

I felt as if the tree had been waiting for me—and for The Aark, the name I had chosen for the wildlife rehabilitation center I was going to open. Originally I intended to spell *Ark* correctly, but someone else was using it, although not in connection with wildlife. "Why don't you spell it A-a-r-k," Debbie suggested. "You never spell anything right, anyway," she giggled. It was a good idea. Adding the second *a* made it okay for us to be The Aark.

Over the years, word of The Aark has spread beyond our

Pennsylvania home into neighboring states. People bring us orphaned and injured birds and wild animals from all over. We try to heal them and return them to their natural habitat. We treat over thirty-five hundred creatures a year, and many of them are young birds who haven't yet flown.

People often ask me how I teach a bird to fly, and my answer always is "I don't. I just give them the opportunity." You do not teach a bird to fly; they fly when they're ready. Some birds, such as swallows, hawks, and Eastern kingbirds, leave the nest in full flight. But most birds need to flutter-fly first. And this is where the fledgling tree comes in.

When I see that our young birds are ready to fly, I begin taking them out of the nursery during the day. I bring them out to the fledgling tree at seven o'clock each morning and put them in two large pens under the tree. The pens are made of wood, with a solid top and back, and wire screening on three sides, which allows plenty of room for several birds to hop around freely. The birds are accustomed to being fed by me, so when I open the pen doors, they come and go as they feed. I don't leave the pens open—I close the doors when I'm finished feeding the birds—but since I feed them every hour until nightfall, they have many opportunities to fly.

The minute a bird flutters up on my shoulder instead of staying on the ground, it begins to stay out for the rest of the day. I take it off my shoulder and put it on the wide branch of the fledgling tree. Some birds will flutter straight up to the tree on their own. If a bird stays on the ground, then it's not ready to fly, so I put it back in the pen and close the door until the next feeding time. It takes a couple of days for most birds to get the hang of flying, but it's important for them to go through the process. It recreates the experience of leaving the nest.

When most birds leave the nest, they flutter-fly from branch to branch, down, then higher up, sometimes hopping, sometimes fluttering, eventually flying. All the while the mother and father birds follow them and feed them, listening for their cries, which they can distinguish from those of any other birds. The babies also know their parents' voices.

Our little orphaned birds know my voice. They associate it with food and protection. When I come out to feed them each hour, I always speak to them. If they aren't already waiting for me on the big branch, they fly down from higher branches. Then I open the pens to see who else wants to leave.

At first the fledglings don't move far from the big branch, but as soon as they have any kind of flight at all, they become real hotshots. Their attitude is "I don't need you—I don't need to be fed." They zoom from the branch to the shrubs to the fence, back and forth, and then they fly higher up into the tree. If they fly too high the first time, they often don't know how to come back down. It may take them all day. But by nighttime, when I bring them all in, they're down. Or, the next morning, when I open the door, there they are, sitting on the step.

In their natural habitat, as fledglings begin to feed themselves, they develop their flying skills. Then the parents stop following them. Instead, the fledglings follow the voices of the parents, and, for a while, even though they can feed themselves, they demand to be fed. If you've ever watched what goes on at a birdfeeder, you'll often see a mother bird feeding a baby that's bigger than she is, and she does it with an attitude of "Oh, all *right!*" Gradually she makes it harder for the baby to get food from her, until finally the baby is on its own. Or, if the baby continues to pester for food, the mother will drive it off or fly away.

When our babies learn to fly well, they also begin to feed

themselves. Quite often they'll bring me the first bug they catch, because they don't know what to do with it. They're very excited about it, but it's all mushy in their mouths. I give it back to them, and then they know what to do with it. After a few more tries, they begin to connect catching the bug with swallowing it. For a while they may still want me to feed them, too, and I do. But finally they leave. Wild things prefer their own habitat. At least most of them do—but there's always the exception.

Spring is the start of The Aark's busy season. Birds and animals begin giving birth, and unfortunate intrusions can threaten the lives of their young. They get hit by cars, and mauled by dogs and cats or by other wild animals. Sometimes they lose a parent before they're old enough to feed themselves. Sometimes a parent abandons them because there isn't enough food to go around—or there's something wrong with the baby. Survival is so chancy in the wild world that there isn't time to fix whatever doesn't work right. But sometimes wildlife rehabbers can help—if we get to the unfortunate ones in time.

A few years ago a woman brought in a very young bluejay. She had found it along the road under a tree, and immediately she knew there was something wrong with it.

"The elbows look funny," she said, pointing to the bird's legs. Instead of being bent back under the bird's body, they stuck out to each side and the bird couldn't stand. "Shouldn't they bend the other way?" the woman asked.

"Actually they're not elbows," I said, "although they do look like them. That part of the leg—from the toes to that elbow-like joint—that's the foot. The elbow-like joint is the heel, and the bird should be squatting down on it."

"Will it be all right?" the woman wanted to know. "Can you help it?"

"Probably," I told her. I asked Rosalie, one of our volunteers, to make out a card for the bird while I took it into the nursery. It was no more than three or four days old, a baby that belonged in a nest. The bird looked kind of naked; its feathers were just coming out of their feather cases. The casings looked like tiny blue straws here and there on the bird's body, and inside each casing was a blue feather. The odd-looking legs were still soft, but they would harden. We had to correct the deformity before the legs hardened in that outlandish position, though, or the bird would never be able to stand. Or fly. Time, vitamins, and proper diet would help, but the most important thing we had to do was recreate a good nest environment.

If you've ever looked into an occupied bird's nest, you probably thought it was too small because the birds were so crowded. They seemed too big for the nest. But when birds are born, they're so floppy that they might as well be put together with rubber bands. They need to be crowded in order to keep their legs under them until they harden in the proper position. Actually, the babies sit on their heels until they grow strong enough to lift themselves up and stand on their toes. If their legs aren't crowded and kept under them while they're soft, they'll stick out to the sides and the bird will be sprawl-legged, just like our little orphan.

I had no way of knowing what went on in its nest. Maybe the mother's other eggs didn't hatch, and the only surviving baby wasn't crowded enough to develop properly. Maybe the mother's food supply was faulty or she had trouble getting enough to feed all her young. In any event, she probably pitched this little one out. In the wild world, that's often the only solution.

I wasn't able to put the bird in an isolette because in those days we had only one and it was already occupied by baby mammals. The next best place for it was a snake box, which is made of wood except for the top and front panels. The top is screened to allow for ventilation and the front is made of glass so the bird or animal can be observed without disturbing it. I put a heating pad in the box and shaped it into a U along the back panel.

Next I folded a diaper and tucked it into a small bread-basket. That was going to be the bluejay's nest. When I placed the bird in it, I made sure that its legs were properly positioned under its body, and then I pulled the diaper up and around its legs, crowding them as if the bird were in its natural nest, sur-rounded by closely-packed siblings. Overcrowding also keeps baby birds warm, and the mother spends a lot of time sitting on them for that same reason, but for now the heating pad would have to do. I put the breadbasket and its only inhabitant in a corner of the box.

Rosalie came in while I was feeding our new patient some of our own recipe for baby birds. "What do you suppose we've got there, a male or a female?" she asked.

I dipped a child's water-color paintbrush into the food and guided it into the gaping mouth. Then I brushed the food against the back of the bird's throat. "We'll have to wait and see," I said. It's impossible to distinguish male from female bluejays. "Unfortunately, it's going to need overhandling."

Ordinarily I don't like to handle our patients any more than absolutely necessary. It makes them too trusting of human be-ings, and it's that much harder for them to make it when they go back into their world. Man is more often an enemy than a friend to wild things, and most wild things know it. Their caution helps them to survive, and I don't like to interfere with it. But we had to check the crowding of the diaper around the bluejay's legs at least every hour, and that meant we would have to handle it more than usual. I hoped that our gentleness would not persuade the bird to give up its wariness about being touched.

The bluejay began to show improvement within four or five days. As its legs hardened under its body, the bird moved its weight forward and squatted on its toes. Its feathers grew out of their cases, covering its body with beautiful shades of blue and gray. Soon it would be ready to fly; the development of a bird from hatch-time to flight is incredibly swift.

I took the baby out to the fledgling tree along with several other young birds, and two days later it was flying and beginning to feed itself. Then it left, and as hard as it was to let the bird go, that was exactly what I wanted it to do. Most of our patients go back into the ecosystem, and we don't know what happens to them there. If you're a sensitive human being, that uncertainty can hurt. Probably half of them will die of natural causes—but that's what they're supposed to do. At least they're not dying because they were hit by a car or because their food supply was wiped out by pesticides or a developer leveling the land. Rehabbers can't *make* wild things live. We can only give them another chance to complete a natural life cycle.

By early fall there were fewer fledglings to bring out to the tree, and soon there were none. The breeding season was over. Finally we brought the pens in and put them away.

One morning late in November I heard a tapping on the dining-room window. I looked out and saw a lovely bluejay. The bird was quite insistent, so I went to the back door, taking a dish of seeds with me. When I opened the door, there was the bird on the step. Without hesitation it came inside. It flew up to my shoulder and then perched on my hand. I poured some seeds in the palm of my other hand and the bird ate some. Most wild birds won't do that. Could it be—? Was it—? I don't pretend to be able to identify one bluejay from another by sight, but sometimes I can distinguish one bird from another by its behavior patterns. And I was certain this was the little sprawl-legged baby bluejay we had healed the past summer. That bird had eaten from my hand, too; in packing the diaper around its legs, I overhandled it so much, that it lost all fear of me.

When the bluejay had enough to eat, it wanted to leave, and I opened the door for it. But the next morning it was back, this time tapping at the kitchen window over the sink where I was rinsing some dishes. I opened the window and in came the bird. It ate and left. It came every day after that, always at the same time and in all kinds of weather.

Then one day it didn't show up. I began looking out the windows on all sides of the house, hoping to catch sight of it. I went out to the fledgling tree but it was empty. I tried not to worry, but I couldn't help myself. Overhandling had its effect on me, too.

Two more days passed and the bluejay didn't come back. Maybe it finally decided to leave for the winter. But maybe—I didn't want to think about other possibilities.

On the fourth day one of my neighbors called me up. "Are you missing a bird?" he asked.

I said, "Is it a bluejay?"

"Yes, yes!" he said. "It's a bluejay. I figured it must be yours because it's doing things I never saw a bluejay do. It comes to my window and taps on it. When I open the window, the bird jumps in. It eats sunflower seeds right out of my hand!"

"Ohmigosh!" I said. I was so relieved.

"I named her Peggy," my neighbor said. "Is that all right?"

"It's lovely," I told him. "But I'm not sure it's a female."

From then on, I called her Peggy, too. So many wild creatures come and go at The Aark that I try not to name them. That way it's easier for me to let them go. Besides, where would I find enough names for the thousands of birds and animals we treat? But Peggy was special. And apparently she wasn't going to leave. At least not that winter.

She began coming back to see me every day, and she continued to visit my neighbor as well. Then another neighbor called to ask me if one of my birds was missing. It seems a bluejay tapped on her window and came inside to eat out of her hand.

"Her name is Peggy," I explained, "and I'm aware that she's gone. It's okay for you to feed her. But, please, don't take her into the house. Let her leave as soon as she wants to." I was concerned that Peggy's new friends might encourage her to stay indoors on a cold or rainy day, and that wasn't a good idea. "When she's ready to go, she's ready, period," I said. "If you don't let her out, she might panic and crash into a window. That could kill her."

Peggy made the rounds that winter, treating all of us to the thrill of having a lovely bird fly down out of the sky, eat out of our hands, and fly off again. My two neighbors lived almost a half-mile away, but Peggy would visit one, then the other, and finally she'd come to The Aark. She was so punctual that I could look at my watch and say, "Well, Peggy's due in." She'd fly in, sit on my hand, and eat some seeds, but she wouldn't allow me to hold her. That was a good sign. Then, early the next spring, we stopped seeing her. This time I wasn't worried. I assumed she was starting a family.

One morning about a month later, when we were setting baby birds on the fledgling tree during the day, I found two little bluejay fledglings sitting on the big branch. I wondered how they got there, because I didn't remember bringing any bluejays out the day before. That upset me. I thought someone had put the birds out there without giving them a chance to go in and out of the pen and be fed. The security of being fed helps the bird to venture into flight. First things first!

The two newcomers took food from me as readily as the other fledglings. As soon as I fed them, I went into the office to look through the admission cards. I was angry. It was a hot day, and I was tired because I had been up most of the night with an injured 'possum. My temper was short. I couldn't find a card for any bluejays, and there were none in the nursery. "Now what?" I thought. "Someone not only left them out there, but didn't even card them in!"

I called in the volunteers and said, "We've got two fledgling bluejays out there, but no card for them. What's the story?"

All I got were puzzled looks and shrugging shoulders. "They should be in the pen before they go on the branch," I told them. I didn't like the sharpness in my voice and tried to tone it down. "I thought you knew that," I said. "It doesn't take much time for them to make the connection, but it's something they absolutely have to do. You can't take shortcuts."

The response was unanimous:

"I didn't put them out there."

"I didn't do it."

"I didn't even know we had any bluejays."

Embarrassment began to replace my anger. I was running out of people, and we still couldn't account for the fledgling bluejays. Frustrated, I went out to the tree again, and there they were, their mouths wide open, ready to eat again.

All of a sudden an adult bluejay came swooping down out of the tree and sat next to the babies. Apparently it was the fledglings' mother. She fed them a bug she had brought with her. Then she sat on my hand and squawked excitedly. She didn't want me to hold her, yet she allowed me to hold the fledglings. It was too much to believe! I was so excited that I thought, "I want this so badly that I'm just making the pieces fit. It can't really be Peggy!"

But I knew it was by the way the bird behaved. She squawked on and on, as if she had so much news to tell me, and then she flew away. She left the fledglings with me. Now, when I was a little girl and my mother needed a break from her kids, she'd take us to Granny's and leave us there for the day. I wondered if bluejay mothers did the same thing. Maybe I was the granny in Peggy's life. I fed the little guys every hour all that day and watched them fly from branch to branch. They were quite accomplished.

It was almost dark when Peggy returned. "Well," I said to her, "did you have a good time?" She sat on my shoulder and then she flew off, taking the fledglings with her. She never brought them back again. But she continued to visit my neighbors and me for a few more winters. Then, last year, we didn't see her. In the wild world, that's often the way good-byes are said.

from THE SWAN IN MY BATHTUB

Good Morning

SHARI SMYTH

One early, ordinary fall morning, I sleepily dragged myself to the deck to shake the kitchen rug. *Yuk!* A cloud of dog hairs and dirt dissolved into my backyard. I turned to go inside, but something out there caught the corner of my eye. On the edge of our pond was a dignified guest, a great heron, standing stock-still on one skinny leg, long sharp beak in profile, as if waiting for its portrait to be finished. Leaning on the railing, I watched it, thrilled at this out-of-the-ordinary, exotic creature visiting my common turf.

Finally, it turned its long beak my way, a spray of head feathers nodding, and gave me a haughty look that said, "Toodle-loo." Spreading enormous wings, it soared over the treetops and on to whatever place it goes for the winter. "Wait!" I wanted to shout. "Stay and be my guest. Live here, so I can thrill to your sight every morning."

I could almost hear it call across the sharp, clean breeze, "How long before I, too, become ordinary?" As I looked around at the wild ducks paddling sparkling wakes in a clear, oval pond, the cloudless sapphire sky spread like a tent pegged with rich crimson trees, the green carpeted field fringed in morning shadows, the calico cat expertly stalking the fence

line, I knew the great heron had been sent to tell me, "Wake up
and see your astonishing backyard!"

Rio's Journey

ANNE WATKINS

---

 stared in dismay at the scuffy green bird gazing back at me from his handmade wire cage. A surprise gift, I didn't know whether to be delighted or horribly upset. He was not much larger than a cockatiel and was dressed in a green suit topped off with dusky blue head feathers. All I knew about him at this point was that he was a blue crowned conure and that he was very sick.

His face was crusted with the thick stuff that oozed from his nostrils. His left eye was swollen and bulged in an ominous way. One wing had been clipped to the bone and the feathers were jagged all the way down to his body! It looked as if someone had used pinking shears on him. He was skinny and breathless and sneezed a lot. Still, there was something about this ragged bundle of feathers that captured my heart.

He climbed to the top of his cage, hung upside down and screeched at me. I couldn't help but laugh, and the more I laughed, the more he clowned.

I didn't know what kind of diseases he might have had and I didn't want my cockatiels and zebra finches to get sick, too, so I immediately quarantined him. I called the local avian vet and made an appointment for my new bird, whom I named Rio.

The next day Rio and I visited the vet's office where I discovered that my poor little guy was in worse shape than I thought. He had a severe sinus infection and an upper respiratory infection, too. To my dismay, the doctor also suspected psittacosis, a nasty, contagious disease that can kill whole flocks of birds!

"I'm sorry," she told me. "I don't think he'll ever recover, and if he does survive, he's so wily, you'll never be able to handle him."

She performed the necessary tests, prescribed the proper antibiotics and vitamins, and made another appointment for us. Armed with instructions on how to catch Rio in a towel so I could work with him, I took my little patient and all his medical paraphernalia home.

Because he was so sick, Rio had to stay in his small blanket-covered travel cage, with a lamp close by for extra warmth. He was so confused and scared! For comfort, I sat next to his cage every available minute and talked to him through the blanket. When our first medication time came later that day, I found a worn-out towel, told myself to get it right the first time, and plunged ahead.

I stuck my hand in the cage, cornered a frenzied Rio and pressed him gently against the bars, careful to keep my fingers out of reach of his slashing beak. Then I tried to pull him out of the cage. Surprise! For such a little fellow, he sure had strong feet. I had to use my other hand to pry his toes off the bars.

I had already filled the dropper with medicine. I wondered how I would pry his beak open if he refused to take it. No problem. He clamped onto the dropper like an alligator. To my relief, he swallowed the nasty brown stuff and ran his tongue around his beak, tasting. It must not have been too bad, because he settled down in my towel-covered hands and gazed calmly back at me.

Over the next few weeks, it became evident that he liked me—and I had already fallen in love with him! He squawked whenever I was out of his sight, and would relax as soon as my towel-covered hand touched his back. His feathers lost some of their raggedness and his nostrils began to clear up. When the test for psittacosis came back negative, we celebrated! Originally given only a 30–40% chance of survival, he was so improved that the doctor was confident that my little patient would recover fully.

By now, Rio was snatching treats from my fingers and rubbing his head against my face. Sometimes he would lick my skin or tug my hair. But we always played by his rules! He could touch me, but I couldn't touch him. If I tried, he warned me with a growl and pin-pointed eyes.

He needed exercise so I began letting Rio out of his cage every day. After a couple of botched attempts, he realized he couldn't fly and contented himself with climbing all over his cage and playing with the toys I made for him. When I wanted him to go back in, all I had to do was show him the towel, and he clambered back inside.

This wild little creature developed a trust in me that touched my heart. This became evident one day when someone he didn't know got too close. In a panic, Rio jumped off his cage onto my arm and ran up to my neck where he huddled, shivering, pressed against me.

Then came the day I had been dreaming of. I was feeding Rio bits of apple and trying to touch his beak each time he took a bite. He ignored my finger and nibbled his treat. I cautiously touched his beak with the tip of my finger. When he didn't try to bite me, I ran my fingertip up to the fringe of dusky blue feathers that edged his nostrils, and gently scratched. Rio dropped his apple, fluffed his feathers and sat very still. Tears of joy streamed down my cheeks as I was finally granted the privilege of touching my precious feathered friend.

Those were the first steps of the long journey from being frightened strangers to becoming trusted friends. Today Rio's feathers are vivid and iridescent; his bright orange and black eyes shine with intelligence and spunk. He demands full body contact—no more of that silly beak touching for him! He solicits tastes of my food by asking "Is it good?" repeatedly until I give in and hand him a sample. He has an interesting vocabulary and loves to sing and dance.

Rio and I have been together for fourteen years now and he is a very special part of my life. It took painstaking months of patience and understanding for us to reach this point but I wouldn't trade a minute of our journey for anything in the world!

Overcoming Obstacles

*"Swimming against the tide,
we find our strengths."*

WILLIAM PETERS

*M*y dog Suzy recently had surgery on her right hind leg after she damaged a ligament while playing. She was in a cast for two weeks, but did that keep her down? Not at all. She seemed to accept the fact that she still had three good legs and managed to get around quite well. I learned something from watching her. Instead of bemoaning what went wrong with our lives, we could try working with what is still right.

Sometimes the best medicine for hard times is to let an animal snuggle up to you and welcome a pat on the head. It's a way of putting things into perspective.

Battle Tactics

FARLEY MOWAT

After several years in Saskatoon, my family moved into a new neighborhood. River Road was on the banks of the Saskatchewan River, but on the lower and more plebian side. The community on River Road was considerably relaxed in character and there was a good deal of tolerance for individual idiosyncrasies.

Only three doors down the street from us lived a retired schoolteacher who had spent years in Alaska and who had brought with him into retirement a team of Alaskan huskies. These were magnificent dogs that commanded respect not only from the local canine population but from the human one as well. Three of them once caught a burglar on their master's premises, and they reduced him to butcher's meat with a dispatch that we youngsters much admired.

Across the alley from us lived a barber who maintained a sort of Transient's Rest for stray mongrels. There was an unkind rumor to the effect that he encouraged these strays only in order to practice his trade upon them. The rumor gained stature from the indisputable fact that some of his oddly assorted collection of dogs sported unusual haircuts. I came to know the barber intimately during the years that followed, and he confided his secret to me. Once, many years earlier, he had seen a

French poodle shaven and shorn, and he had been convinced that he could devise even more spectacular hair styles for dogs, and perhaps make a fortune and a reputation for himself. His experiments were not without artistic merit, even though some of them resulted in visits from the Humane Society inspectors.

I had no trouble fitting myself into this new community, but the adjustment was not so simple for Mutt. The canine population of River Road was enormous. Mutt had to come to terms with these dogs, and he found the going hard. His long, silken hair and his fine "feathers" tended to give him a soft and sentimental look that was misleading and that seemed to goad the roughneck local dogs into active hostility. They usually went about in packs, and the largest pack was led by a well-built bull terrier who lived next door to us. Mutt, who was never a joiner, preferred to go his way alone, and this made him particularly suspect by the other dogs. They began to lay for him.

He was not by nature the fighting kind. In all his life I never knew him to engage in battle unless there was no alternative. His was an eminently civilized attitude, but one that other dogs could seldom understand. They taunted him because of it.

His pacific attitude used to embarrass my mother when the two of them happened to encounter a belligerent strange dog while they were out walking. Mutt would waste no time in idle braggadocio. At first glimpse of the stranger he would insinuate himself under Mother's skirt and no amount of physical force, nor scathing comment, could budge him from this sanctuary. Often the strange dog would not realize that it *was* a sanctuary and this was sometimes rather hard on Mother.

Despite his repugnance toward fighting, Mutt was no coward, nor was he unable to defend himself. He had his own ideas about how to fight, ideas which were unique but formidable. Just how efficacious they actually were was demonstrated to us all within a week of our arrival at our new address.

Knowing nothing of the neighborhood, Mutt dared to go where even bulldogs feared to tread, and one morning he foolishly pursued a cat into the ex-schoolteacher's yard. He was immediately surrounded by four ravening huskies. They were a merciless lot, and they closed in for the kill.

Mutt saw at once that this time he would have to fight. With one quick motion he flung himself over on his back and began to pedal furiously with all four feet. It looked rather as if he were riding a bicycle built for two, but upside down. He also began to sound his siren. This was a noise he made—just how I do not know—deep in the back of his throat. It was a kind of frenzied wail. The siren rose in pitch and volume as his legs increased their r.p.m.'s, until he began to sound like a gas turbine at full throttle.

The effect of this unorthodox behavior on the four huskies was to bring them to an abrupt halt. Their ears went forward and their tails uncurled as a look of pained bewilderment wrinkled their brows. And then slowly, and one by one, they began to back away, their eyes uneasily averted from the distressing spectacle before them. When they were ten feet from Mutt they turned as one dog and fled without dignity for their own back yard.

The mere sight of Mutt's bicycle tactics (as we referred to them) was usually sufficient to avert bloodshed, but on occasion a foolhardy dog would refuse to be intimidated. The results in these cases could be rather frightful, for Mutt's queer posture of defense was not all empty bombast.

Once when we were out hunting gophers Mutt was attacked by a farm collie who, I think, was slightly mad. He looked mad, for he had one white eye and one blue one, and the combination gave him a maniac expression. And he acted mad, for he flung himself on the inverted Mutt without the slightest hesitation.

Mutt grunted when the collie came down on top of him, and for an instant the tempo of his legs was slowed. Then he exerted himself and, as it were, put on a sprint. The collie became air-borne, bouncing up and down as a rubber ball bounces on the end of a water jet. Each time he came down he was raked fore and aft by four sets of rapidly moving claws, and when he finally fell clear he was bleeding from a dozen ugly scratches, and he had had a bellyful. He fled. Mutt did not pursue him; he was magnanimous in victory.

Had he been willing to engage deliberately in a few such duels with the neighborhood dogs, Mutt would undoubtedly have won their quick acceptance. But such was his belief in the principles of nonviolence—as these applied to other dogs, at least—that he continued to avoid combat.

The local packs, and particularly the one led by the bull terrier next door, spared no pains to bring him to battle, and for some time he was forced to stay very close to home unless he was accompanied by Mother or by myself. It was nearly a month before he found a solution to this problem.

The solution he eventually adopted was typical of him.

Almost all the back yards in Saskatoon were fenced with vertical planking nailed to horizontal two-by-fours. The upper two-by-four in each case was usually five or six feet above the ground, and about five inches below the projecting tops of the upright planks. For generations these elevated gangways had provided a safe thoroughfare for cats. One fine day Mutt decided that they could serve him too.

I was brushing my teeth after breakfast when I heard Mutt

give a yelp of pain and I went at once to the window and looked out. I was in time to see him laboriously clamber up on our back fence from a garbage pail that stood by the yard gate. As I watched he wobbled a few steps along the upper two-by-four, lost his balance, and fell off. Undaunted he returned at once to the garbage pail and tried again.

I went outside and tried to reason with him, but he ignored me. When I left he was still at it, climbing up, staggering along for a few feet, then falling off again.

I mentioned this new interest of his during dinner that night, but none of us gave it much thought. We were used to Mutt's peculiarities, and we had no suspicion that there was method behind this apparent foolishness. Yet method there was, as I discovered a few evenings later.

A squad of Bengal lancers, consisting of two of my friends and myself armed with spears made from bamboo fishing rods, had spent the afternoon riding up and down the back alleys on our bicycles hunting tigers (alley cats). As suppertime approached we were slowly pedaling our way homeward along the alley behind River Road when one of my chums, who was a little in the lead, gave a startled yelp and swerved his bike so that I crashed into him, and we fell together on the sun-baked dirt. I picked myself up and saw my friend pointing at the fence ahead of us. His eyes were big with disbelief.

The cause of the accident, and of my chum's incredulity, was nonchalantly picking his way along the top of the fence not fifty yards away. Behind that fence lay the home of the huskies, and although we could not see them, we—and most of Saskatoon—could hear them. Their frenzied howls were punctuated by dull thudding sounds as they leaped at their tormentor and fell back helplessly to earth again.

Mutt never hesitated. He ambled along his aerial route with the leisurely insouciance of an old gentleman out for an evening stroll. The huskies must have been wild with frustration, and I was grateful that the fence lay between them and us.

We three boys had not recovered from our initial surprise when a new canine contingent arrived upon the scene. It included six or seven of the local dogs (headed by the bull terrier) attracted to the scene by the yammering of the huskies. They spotted Mutt, and the terrier immediately led a mass assault. He launched himself against the fence with such foolhardy violence that only a bull terrier could have survived the impact.

We were somewhat intimidated by the frenzy of all those dogs, and we lowered our spears to the "ready" position, undecided whether to attempt Mutt's rescue or not. In any event, we were not needed.

Mutt remained unperturbed, although this may have been only an illusion resulting from the fact that he was concentrating so hard on his balancing act that he could spare no attention for his assailants. He moved along at a slow but steady pace, and having safely navigated the huskies' fence, he jumped up to the slightly higher fence next door and stepped along it until he came to a garage. With a graceful leap he gained the garage roof, where he lay down for a few moments, ostensibly to rest, but actually—I am certain—to enjoy his triumph.

Below him there was pandemonium. I have never seen a dog as angry as that bull terrier was. Although the garage wall facing on the alley was a good eight feet high, the terrier kept hurling himself impotently against it until he must have been one large quivering bruise.

Mutt watched the performance for two or three minutes;

then he stood up and with one insolent backward glance jumped down to the dividing fence between two houses, and ambled along it to the street front beyond.

The tumult in the alley subsided and the pack began to disperse. Most of the dogs must have realized that they would have to run halfway around the block to regain Mutt's trail, and by then he might be far away. Dispiritedly they began to drift off, until finally only the bull terrier remained. He was still hurling himself at the garage wall in a paroxysm of fury when I took myself home to tell of the wonders I had seen.

From that day forth the dogs of the neighborhood gave up their attempts against Mutt and came to a tacit acceptance of him—all, that is, save the bull terrier. Perhaps his handball game against the fence had addled his brain, or it may be that he was just too stubborn to give up. At any rate he continued to lurk in ambush for Mutt, and Mutt continued to avoid him easily enough, until the early winter when the terrier—by now completely unbalanced—one day attempted to cross the street in pursuit of his enemy and without bothering to look for traffic. He was run over by an old Model T.

Mutt's remarkable skill as a fence walker could have led to the leadership of the neighborhood dogs, had that been what he desired, for his unique talent gave him a considerable edge in the popular game of catch-cat; but Mutt remained a lone walker, content to be left to his own devices.

He did not give up fence walking even when the original need had passed. He took a deep pride in his accomplishment, and he kept in practice. I used to show him off to my friends, and I was not above making small bets with strange boys about the abilities of my acrobatic dog. When I won, as I always did, I would reward Mutt with candy-coated gum. This was one of his favorite confections and he would chew away at a wad of it until the last vestige of mint flavor had vanished, whereupon he would swallow the tasteless remnant. Mother thought that this was bad for him, but as far as I know, it never had any adverse effect upon his digestive system, which could absorb most things with impunity.

from THE DOG WHO WOULDN'T BE

A Dog-Gone Case

NANCY B. GIBBS

I'll never forget the summer after the first grade. My brother, Neal, had become very ill after contracting scarlet fever.

Our family pet, Blue, was a beautiful Belgian police dog who possessed many qualities admired by all dog lovers. Although she was protective of her family and a lady in all regards, her best quality was the unconditional love that she had for us. As my brother spent much of the time in the bed recuperating, Blue stayed by his side, both day and night. After several weeks of confinement, Neal finally began feeling better.

Early one morning, during breakfast, our doorbell rang. I threw down my cereal spoon and ran to the front door. Blue ran ahead of me. She was growling and barking uncontrollably. She had never acted like that before, so we were very surprised. I later realized that she had apparently sensed something that we didn't understand at the time.

My mother grabbed Blue's collar and went to the back of the house with her. Blue snarled all the way to the bedroom. As I opened the door, I saw a husky, unshaved man standing on the porch with a solemn expression on his face. "I'd like to see your mother," he said sharply.

Mom quickly came to the door. "I want my dog!" the man shouted. "Either give me my dog, or two hundred dollars by two o'clock today, or I'll have you arrested." Then he turned and walked away, without giving my mother a chance to respond.

Blue was the only dog we had. She had been a part of our family for quite a few years. Mom had no idea who the man was, what his dog looked like, or where his dog was. Fear overcame her, however, and she immediately called my father at work.

"Don't worry about it," Daddy said. "You don't have his dog. We're not giving him any money. I'm sure that you will never hear from him again. Just don't worry."

I sensed that she was still upset. She had heard the tone of the man's voice and seen the bitterness in his eyes. For our sakes, however, she tried to ignore what had just happened. When she allowed Blue to come out of the bedroom, Blue whined and paced in front of the door. She didn't settle down for hours.

A few days later, our doorbell rang again. I looked out the front window and there stood a policeman. I saw his gun strapped around his waist.

Neal and I began to cry. I realized that my mother was being arrested. The policeman allowed her to call a relative to come and stay with us before they took her to jail.

During the time Mom was gone, Blue stayed close to me. She was a wonderful companion, as I sobbed uncontrollably. She constantly licked my cheeks trying to wash away the tears and the pain of seeing my mother taken to jail for a crime she didn't commit.

A few hours later, Mom returned home with Daddy. She was hysterical after going through such an ordeal. Little did I know, at the age of seven, how much grief we would experience over the next two years.

We spent hours in lawyers' offices and courtrooms. My brother and I were kept out of school to testify in court. My brother's doctor was present. Our neighbors, my mother's boss and all of our relatives were summoned to court, as well. Many newspaper headlines across America read, "A Dog-Gone Case." Our lives had become a soap opera, and a crazy one at that.

In the meantime the man found his dog. Both his dog and Blue went to court. While the other dog acted unruly, Blue remained calm and behaved like a lady during the trial. When my father led Blue into the courtroom, she spotted my mother. She ran and jumped into her lap while Mom sat on the witness stand.

When I was allowed out of the witness room, I stopped to look inside the courtroom while Mom was being questioned. She was crying bitterly, and Blue licked her face, just as she had while consoling me the day the ordeal began. Blue hated to see any of us cry.

The jurors reached out to pet Blue, but she continued to stare at my mother, ignoring everyone else in the courtroom. There wasn't a dry eye in the juror's box as they watched the compassion and devotion Blue showed for my mother during that difficult time. The more my mother cried, the closer Blue got to her.

Needless to say, my mother's name was cleared, but it took a long time for our family to recover from such a horrible experience. Throughout it all, Blue was there for us, every step of the way. She taught us a great deal about how to comfort the ones you love when life just doesn't seem fair.

Persisto, the Squirrel

KAREN KING MURPHY

$\mathcal{T}$he gray squirrel took a running leap and shinnied up the thin metal pole. His destination: our home-made bird feeder. With his front paws, the bushy-tailed rodent tipped the small platform to one side and climbed on board for a tasty snack. Seeds flew in every direction. After getting word to his frisky buddies, more squirrels took turns at the free food. Twenty pounds of seed, a can of WD40, an industrial size jar of petroleum jelly, and several other "deterrents" bit the dust before my husband decided it was time to purchase a different bird feeder. Little did I know the acquisition would result in answered prayer.

For several months I had been struggling with self-doubt involving a personal ambition. The more I worked on, thought about, and prayed for the aspiration to become reality, the more it seemed to elude me. My head told me to give up and get on with battling life's trials, without adding another burden. Let the dream go. Yet God's continual, blessed nearness to me during breast cancer surgery and chemotherapy treatment increased my desire to minister by the medium of written words.

James, chapter 1:2-4, says, "Consider it pure joy, my brothers, whenever you face trials of many kinds, because you know that the testing of your faith develops perseverance. Perseverance must finish its work so that you may be mature and complete, not lacking anything." This scripture verse, the lowly squirrel outside my window, and our new bird feeder all served to teach me a lesson.

Shopping for the bird feeder proved to be an eye-opening experience, especially since they came in so many shapes and sizes. Some touted themselves as exactly what we needed—"squirrel-proof." We bought one, took it home, and hung it on the skinny pole's hook.

It didn't take long for squirrel reconnaissance moves to begin. All, except one, admitted defeat after two days of intensive work trying to get the seeds. The persistent one kept at it. He used our deck's railing as a launching point, jumping to the feeder's roof many times a day. The slope and smooth surface dumped him unceremoniously on the ground every time. Still determined, he started scuffing his little paws in dirt, much as a baseball batter does who wants more grip. Now he could hold on to the slippery roof's surface, hang upside down by his back paws, and stretch toward the bird seed. Alas, when his front paws touched the open seed ports, the weight-sensitive flap closed. Result—no food!

After watching a week of unsuccessful squirrel maneuvers, my husband and I congratulated each other for finding the most effective pest-proof bird feeder. However, we underestimated the creature. He wasn't deterred.

The next day during our breakfast time, "Persisto, the Squirrel" returned. He ran along the deck's railing and stopped in front of the feeder. He sat for a minute eyeing it, then reared onto his back legs, and pitched forward horizontally. In this precarious position, with his front paws holding the corner of the feeder, he pulled it toward himself. Without any weight on the sensitive flap, he craned his neck around the edge. "Persisto" nibbled contentedly—task accomplished.

The squirrel's shenanigans earned my grudging admiration. His persistence prompted me to ask important self-evaluative questions: Had I truly put all my effort into making my hopes become reality? Was I giving up my dream too easily because of discouragement? Did perceived difficulties make me run off looking for easier, greener pastures?

The advantages of sticking with a project until it was completed were apparent, but somewhere along the way my resolve had gotten sidetracked. Thumbing through my Bible, I came across Psalm 105:4 that says, "Look to the Lord and his strength; seek his face always." Here was a gentle reminder that I had been relying upon myself to get the job done, not looking to the Lord for his direction. The word "always" brought to my mind the squirrel who diligently sought every avenue open to him. After each unsuccessful attempt he tried again, finally achieving the victory he sought.

Before me lay the answer to my prayers. Writing words that uplift and encourage others to put their faith and trust in God and glorify His name, even under difficult circumstances, can be accomplished with persistence. Most importantly, I must look to the Lord's strength in this important endeavor.

With God's help and patient persistence on my part, I believe the effort to make a positive difference in others' lives through writing will succeed. Just as the squirrel worked hard and did not give up until he had achieved his goal, neither will I.

A Memorable Battle

FRED BAUER

While visiting our son Chris in Anchorage last year, Shirley and I got to see some of Alaska's most beautiful scenery—Denali National Park (Mt. McKinley), Resurrection Bay and Prince William Sound, for starters. But it was on a boat trip at the latter that I saw something more memorable than all the glaciers, grizzly bears, mountain goats, caribou, moose, bald eagles, kittiwakes and horned puffins.

The incident pitted a giant eagle against a tiny mother murrelet, a mottled brown waterfowl, and her brood. The diving bird of prey swooped down again and again on Mama and the four chicks that paddled behind her. Dozens of us watched from railside, riveted by the David-and-Goliath drama. On each pass I held my breath, sure the eagle would snag one of the babies with its lethal talons. But every time the eagle dove, the intrepid mother signaled impending danger and in unison they went submarine. Then like corks they popped up and swam on. Eventually, the frustrated eagle gave up and flew off.

I applauded Mother Murrelet's courage. But it took more than courage to save her chicks. It took discipline. Sometime earlier she had taught her offspring to obey her. I could imagine that in quiet bays and eddies she had schooled them to follow her instructions. Because they did, they lived to swim another day.

I need to remember this lesson when I grow inconsistent in my spiritual pilgrimage, forgetting to pray and study God's Word. It is that discipline in good times that prepares me for bad, which will come to all of us as surely as the seasons. The difference is that in adversity, I'll know Whom to call on and—with absolute certainty—Who will answer.

How Kato Was Rescued

GRAHAM PHALEN

The five of us worked to fit the horse's legs through the holes of the cargo net while trying to maintain our footing on the treacherously muddy ledge. Kato, the horse, tossed his head and nervously nipped at Duane, who struggled to keep him still.

The horse could sense our urgency. Though we worked quietly and smoothly, placing his tired, shaking legs through the net, we had to be communicating our concern to the exhausted animal. The clouds were closing in rapidly, obscuring the buttes around us. We had only a few minutes to accomplish our task; Kato's ordeal had lasted seven days, and in trying to bring it to a close, we had to do everything right the first time. We might not get a second chance.

It began the previous Sunday, when John Hoffman and two friends rode their horses into the Superstition Mountain Wilderness Area, located roughly fifty miles east of Phoenix, Arizona. They took a wrong turn on the rugged trail. The terrain would have been difficult at best for a skilled hiker; it was extremely taxing for the horses. They came to a bald rock face with a narrow defile cutting down the steep slope. It appeared tricky but passable from where they stood.

It wasn't that easy though. Fifty feet below the trail, they were unable to lead their horses any farther. The rock became smooth and slippery, and below stretched an impassable, barren sandstone grade.

The riders were able to drive two of the horses back up to the trail, but John Hoffman's 1200-pound sorrel gelding, Kato, couldn't make it.

Hoffman and his friends stayed on the mountain two days and two nights, repeatedly trying to urge the horse up the narrow crevice, but Kato's spirit flagged. He only ended up abraded and defeated by the climb.

On Wednesday, Hoffman called me to request the help of the Arizona Humane Society. I organized a small group of volunteers, and we hiked an adjoining trail, Route 233, with him that afternoon. The climb was tough, with thirty- to forty-pound packs of food and water on our backs, but it was worth every step when we saw Kato eagerly eat his rations.

Thursday was much the same. We packed supplies up the two-mile trail that morning, and spent the day improving the steep grade and poor footing the horse would have to climb. Kato ate and rested on a small shelf below the slide. Although he had sustained minor leg injuries, his attitude had improved by late that afternoon.

Friday, a group of fifteen volunteers, including five volunteers from the Central Arizona Mountain Rescue Association, attempted to assist Kato up the cleft using a system of pulleys and an improvised harness. With five of us working with the horse and the rest on the ropes, we managed to get Kato twenty feet up the base of the climb, but could not urge him farther. Despite long periods of rest and a slow pace, the combination of stress and exhaustion took its toll. He would approach the climb, leaning for support on the harness, only to collapse on his side with a groan. Leg wraps kept him from injuring himself seriously, but we decided not to risk overstressing him. While our veterinarian, Dr. Carol Spillers, examined Kato, Jerry Foster from local television station KPNX helicoptered in on SKY 12 and dropped us some supplies. He felt we could have the horse airlifted out. We agreed to try the lift Saturday morning, and left Kato eating his ration of alfalfa pellets.

Saturday was a discouraging day. The Superstitions were completely socked in with heavy fog and rain. Foster, flying SKY 12, and pilot Gary Mercer, flying a helicopter donated by Air Services International, were unable to fly with the low ceiling, but stayed on standby in case of a break in the weather.

A small group of us once more ascended the trail, equipped with food and water. The trek was made doubly difficult with constant rain, dense fog, slippery rock, and soggy clothing. I reasoned that if I was uncomfortable, Kato had to be miserable.

When we reached Kato's ledge, we found him soaked and shivering, standing on what was now a slippery incline of mud and water. We rubbed him down and made a makeshift blanket out of Foster's cargo net and sheets and ponchos of plastic. We waited for a break in the weather while Kato warmed up and ate, but realized that, with ice particles floating through the fog and a ten-mile-per-hour wind, hypothermia was a real possibility for our team. I left Kato to stay one more night on the soggy little ledge, wrapped as warmly as we could make him.

Sunday arrived with much the same weather. Low clouds and rain swirled intermittently around the sandstone knob where Kato was trapped. Dr. Spillers felt that Kato couldn't take much more exposure. We had to get him out that day;

another storm was reported on its way. We called in our two volunteer pilots, while fourteen members of the Apache Junction Helicopter Rescue Team stood by to assist in the lift attempt. At around 10:15 A.M., the clouds began to break around the summit.

We scrambled to take advantage of the break and quickly assembled the rescue team. Jerry Foster airlifted Dr. Spillers to the landing zone, followed by Arizona Humane Society Lieutenant Duane Adams and myself. We were to handle the horse. Apache Junction Mountain Rescue's Gene Berry and Art Tice were flown up to assist us.

Kato was fairly dry, but tired and shaking from standing on the muddy ledge. He had become entangled in his muddy blanket, and we had a few anxious moments unwrapping him while he struggled to maintain his balance.

We faced the most difficult part of our task. While maneuvering on the narrow, slippery perch, we were to position the horse in the net so that he would be properly balanced for the airship, unable to fall forward or backward during the flight, and be able to breathe properly. If he slipped or went down in the mud while we positioned the net, we were sunk. If he spooked or fussed, he could send us flying off the narrow shelf or seriously injure us. The pilot would lift the horse slightly to test the load, but we would probably only have one real chance. The weather was worsening.

We positioned the center of the net under Kato's girth, in line with his withers. We then placed his front legs through the holes in the net, careful not to risk splaying his legs or cutting off his wind at the neck. Duane, at the horse's head, quieted him as we placed his rear legs through. We were forced to cut the webbing to get the net over his hocks. He fidgeted and fought to get his footing on the slick incline. We had to be careful not to compromise the integrity of the net. After ten minutes of careful work, we were finished.

Next was a crucial step in the mission. Dr. Spillers was flown back to base camp, where John Hoffman, Kato's owner, and several volunteers waited to receive the horse. Gary Mercer, piloting Air Services International's Bell Long Ranger helicopter, lifted off and ascended with Jerry Foster in SKY 12 alongside, to relay radio instructions.

On the ledge, the four of us watched the choppers approach. Gene guided them by radio, while Art, Duane and I positioned the net and steadied the horse. After the initial gust from the rotor wash, Mercer expertly placed the end of the 100-foot cargo cable on the nearby rock to ground out its charge. After the flight up, the cable had collected enough static electricity to knock a man off his feet.

Despite all the strange noise and activity, Kato remained fairly quiet. We passed the hook through the four corner rings, while Mercer held his ship and the cable rock-steady. The slack was gently taken up until the net was almost taut.

Gene gave the thumbs up signal, and Mercer gently lifted Kato upwards. He was startled, but after a few minor crow hops, he was lifted a couple of feet off the ground to hang placidly.

We all looked at each other and instantly agreed: we had to do it, now. The thick clouds were rolling in fast; there wouldn't be another chance. With cries of "Go! Go! Go!" we signaled the pilot up, and Kato was on his way. The horse remained calm and quiet in the net, looking around curiously as he was gradually carried down the valley in a low level flight.

As I climbed along the rock face to watch their descent, I experienced a great surge of elation and relief. We weren't out of the woods yet, but at least the exhausted animal was on his way down.

Then came the voice over the radio: "Kato is down and OK!" We all cheered, shaking hands and grinning ear to ear, ecstatic at the good news. I don't think I've ever felt so good.

After the flight from the mountain back to meet our exhilarated group on the ground, I looked up the valley and saw clouds once again obscuring the knob. I reflected on our good fortune. A potentially dangerous and risky operation had ended in triumph. Our friend was back on level ground, contentedly munching hay, his happy owner smiling quietly by his side. With the hard work, commitment and cooperation of some dedicated volunteers, and the care and skill of two fine helicopter pilots, we had done it. Kato was safe.

from CIRCLES OF COMPASSION

Snap

ERNEST THOMPSON SETON

It was dusk on Hallowe'en when first I saw him. Early in the morning I had received a telegram from my college chum Jack: "Lest we forget. Am sending you a remarkable pup. Be polite to him; it's safer." It would have been just like Jack to have sent an infernal machine or a skunk rampant and called it a pup, so I awaited the hamper with curiosity. When it arrived I saw it was marked "dangerous," and there came from within a high-pitched snarl at every slight provocation. On peering through the wire netting I saw it was not a baby tiger but a small white bull terrier. He snapped at me and at anyone or anything that seemed too abrupt or too near for proper respect, and his snarling growl was unpleasantly frequent. Dogs have two growls: one deep-rumbled and chesty; that is polite warning— the retort courteous, the other mouthy and much higher in pitch. This is the last word before actual onslaught. The terrier's growls were all of the latter kind. I was a dog man and thought I knew all about dogs. So, dismissing the porter, I got out my all-round jackknife-toothpick-nailhammer-hatchet-toolbox-fire-shovel. It's a specialty of our firm, and lifted the netting. Oh yes, I knew all about dogs. The little fury had been growling out a whole-souled growl for every tap of the tool, and when I turned the box on its side he made a dash straight for my legs. Had not his foot gone through the wire netting and held him, I might have been hurt, for his heart was evidently in his work; but I stepped on the table out of reach and tried to reason with him. I have always believed in talking to animals. I maintain that they gather something of our intention at least, even if they do not understand our words; but the dog evidently put me down for a hypocrite and scorned my approaches. At first he took his post under the table and kept up a circular watch for a leg trying to get down.

I could have controlled him with my eye, but couldn't bring it to bear where I was, or rather where he was. Thus I was left a prisoner. I am a very cool person, I flatter myself; in fact, I represent a hardware firm, and in coolness we are not excelled. I got out a cigar and smoked tailor style on the table while my little tyrant below kept watch for legs. I got out the telegram and read it: "Remarkable pup. Be polite to him; it's safer." I think it was my coolness rather than my politeness that did it, for in half an hour the growling ceased. In an hour he no longer jumped at a newspaper cautiously pushed over the edge to test his humor; possibly the irritation of the cage was wearing off. By the time I had lit my third cigar he waddled out to the fire and lay down, not ignoring me, however. I had no reason to complain of that kind of contempt. He kept one eye on me, and I kept both eyes, not on him, but on his stumpy tail. If that tail should swing sidewise once, I should feel I was winning; but it did not swing. I got a book and put in time on that table till my legs were cramped and the fire burned low. About 10 P.M. it was chilly, and at half-past ten the fire was out. My Hallowe'en present got up, yawned and stretched, then walked under my bed, where he found a fur rug. By stepping lightly from the table to the dresser and then onto the mantelshelf I also reached bed, and very quietly undressing, got in without provoking any criticism from my master. I had not yet fallen asleep when I heard a slight scrambling and felt "thump-thump" on the bed, then over my feet and legs; Snap evidently had found it too cool down below, and proposed to have the best my house afforded.

He curled up on my feet in such a way that I was very uncomfortable and tried to readjust matters, but the slightest wriggle of my toe was enough to make him snap at it so fiercely that nothing but thick woolen bedclothes saved me from being maimed for life.

I was an hour moving my feet—a hair's breadth at a time—till they were so that I could sleep in comfort; and I was awakened several times during the night by angry snarls from the dog—I suppose because I dared to move a toe without his approval, though once I believe he did it simply because I was snoring.

In the morning I was ready to get up before Snap was. You see, I called him Snap—Gingersnap in full. Some dogs are hard to name and some do not seem to need it—they name themselves.

I was ready to rise at seven. Snap was not ready till eight, so we rose at eight. He had little to say to the man who made the fire. He allowed me to dress without doing it on the table. As I left the room to get breakfast, I remarked:

"Snap, my friend, some men would whip you into a different way, but I think I know a better plan. The doctors nowadays favor the 'no-breakfast cure.' I shall try that."

It seemed cruel, but I left him without food all day. It cost me something to repaint the door where he scratched it, but at night he was quite ready to accept a little food at my hands.

In a week we were very good friends. He would sleep on my bed now and allow me to move my feet without snapping at them, intent to do me serious bodily harm. The no-breakfast cure had worked wonders; in three months we were—well, simply man and dog, and he amply justified the telegram he came with.

He seemed to be without fear. If a small dog came near, he would take not the slightest notice; if a medium-sized dog, he would stick his stub of a tail rigidly up in the air, then walk around him, scratching contemptuously with his hind feet and looking at the sky, the distance, the ground, anything but the dog, and noting his presence only by frequent high-pitched growls. If the stranger did not move on at once the battle began, and then the stranger usually moved on very rapidly. Snap sometimes got worsted, but no amount of sad experience could ever inspire him with a grain of caution. Once, while riding in a cab during the dog show, Snap caught sight of an elephantine St. Bernard taking an airing. Its size aroused such enthusiasm in the pup's little breast that he leaped from the cab window to do battle and broke his leg.

Evidently fear had been left out of his make-up and its place supplied with an extra amount of ginger, the reason for his full name. He differed from all other dogs I have ever known. For example, if a boy threw a stone at him he ran, not away, but toward the boy, and if the crime was repeated Snap took the law into his own hands; thus he was at least respected by all. Only myself and the porter at the office seemed to realize his good points, and we only were admitted to the high honor of personal friendship, an honor which I appreciated more as months went on. By midsummer not Carnegie, Vanderbilt and Astor together could have raised money enough to buy a quarter of a share in my little dog Snap.

Though not a regular traveler, I was ordered out on the road in the autumn, and then Snap and the landlady were left together, with unfortunate developments. Contempt on his part, fear on hers, and hate on both.

I was placing a lot of barbed wire in the northern tier of states. My letters were forwarded once a week, and I got several complaints from the landlady about Snap.

When I arrived at Mendoza, in North Dakota, I found a fine market for wire. Of course my dealings were with the big storekeepers, but I went about among the ranchmen to get their practical views on the different styles, and thus I met the Penroof Brothers' cow outfit.

One could be long in cow country without hearing a great deal about the depredations of the ever wily and destructive gray wolf. The day had gone by when they could be poisoned wholesale, and they were a serious drain on the rancher's profits. The Penroof brothers, like most live cattlemen, had given up all attempts at poisoning and trapping, and were trying various breeds of dogs as wolf hunters, hoping to get a little sport out of the necessary work of destroying the pests.

Foxhounds had failed—they were too soft for fighting. Great Danes were too clumsy, and greyhounds could not follow the game unless they could see it. Each breed had some fatal defect, but the cowmen hoped to succeed with a mixed pack, and the day when I was invited to join in a Mendoza wolf-hunt, I was amused by the variety of dogs that followed. There were several mongrels, but there were also a few highly bred dogs—in particular, some Russian wolfhounds that must have cost a lot of money.

Hilton Penroof, the oldest boy, "The Master of Hounds," was

unusually proud of them and expected them to do great things.

"Greyhounds are too thin-skinned to fight a wolf, Danes are too slow, but you'll see the fur fly when the Russians take a hand."

Thus the greyhounds were there as runners, the Danes as heavy backers, and the Russians to do the important fighting. There were also two or three foxhounds, whose fine noses were relied on to follow the trail if the game got out of view.

It was a fine sight as we rode away among the Badland Buttes that October day. The air was bright and crisp, and though so late, there was neither snow nor frost. The horses were fresh, and once or twice showed me how a cow pony tries to get rid of his rider.

The dogs were keen for sport, and we did start one or two gray spots in the plain that Hilton said were wolves or coyotes. The dogs trailed away at full cry, but at night, beyond the fact that one of the greyhounds had a wound on his shoulder, there was nothing to show that any of them had been on a wolf-hunt.

"It's my opinion yer fancy Russians is no good, Hilt," said Garvin, the younger brother. "I'll back that little black Dane against the lot, mongrel an' all as he is."

"I don't unnerstan' it," growled Hilton. "There ain't a coyote, let alone a gray wolf, kin run away from them greyhounds; them foxhounds kin folly a trail three days old, an' the Danes could lick a grizzly."

"I reckon," said the father, "they kin run, an' they kin track, an' they kin lick a grizzly, *maybe,* but the fac' is they don't want to tackle a gray wolf. The hull darn pack is scairt—an' I wish we had our money out o' them."

Thus the men grumbled and discussed as I drove away and left them.

There seemed only one solution of the failure. The hounds were swift and strong, but a gray wolf seems to terrorize all dogs. They have not the nerve to face him, and so each time he gets away.

My thoughts flew back to the fearless little dog that had shared my bed for the last year. How I wished he was out here. Then these lubberly giants of hounds would find a leader whose nerve would not fail at the moment of trial.

At Baroka, my next stop, I got a batch of mail including two letters from the landlady; the first to say that "that beast of a dog was acting up scandalous in my room," and the other still more forcible, demanding his immediate removal.

"Why not have him expressed to Mendoza?" I thought. "It's only twenty hours; they'll be glad to have him. I can take him home with me when I go through."

My next meeting with Gingersnap was not as different from the first as one might have expected. He jumped on me, made much vigorous pretense to bite, and growled frequently, but it was a deep-chested growl and his stump was wagging very hard.

The Penroofs had had a number of wolf-hunts since I was with them, and were much disgusted at having no better success than before. The dogs could find a wolf nearly every time they went out, but they could not kill him, and the men were not near enough at the finish to learn why.

Old Penroof was satisfied that "thar wasn't one of the hull miserable gang that had the grit of a jack-rabbit."

We were off at dawn the next day—the same procession of fine horses and superb riders, and the big blue dogs, the yellow dogs, the spotted dogs, as before: But there was a new feature, a little white dog that stayed close by me, and not only any dogs, but horses that came too near were apt to get a surprise from his teeth. I think he quarrelled with every man, horse and dog in the country, with the exception of a bull terrier belonging to the Mendoza hotel man. She was the only one smaller than himself, and they seemed very good friends.

I shall never forget the view of the hunt I had that day. We were on one of those large, flat-headed buttes that give a kingdom to the eye, when Hilton, who had been scanning the vast country with glasses, exclaimed: "I see him. There he goes, toward Skull Creek. Guess it's a coyote."

Now the first thing is to get the greyhounds to see the prey—not an easy matter, as they cannot use the glasses, and the ground was covered with sage brush higher than the dogs' heads.

But Hilton called, "Hu, hu, Dander," and leaned aside from his saddle, holding out his foot at the same time. With one agile bound Dander leaped to the saddle and there stood balancing on the horse while Hilton kept pointing. "There he is, Dander; sic him—see him down there." The dog gazed earnestly where his master pointed, then seeming to see, he sprang to the ground with a slight yelp and sped away. The other dogs followed after, in an ever-lengthening procession, and we rode as hard as we could behind them, but losing time, for the ground was cut with gullies, spotted with badger holes, and covered with rocks and sage that made full speed too hazardous.

We all fell behind, and I was last, of course, being least accustomed to the saddle. We got several glimpses of the dogs flying over the level plain or dropping from sight in gullies to reappear at the other side. Dander, the greyhound, was the recognized leader, and as we mounted another ridge we got sight of the whole chase—a coyote at full speed, the dogs a quarter of a mile behind, but gaining. When next we saw them the coyote was dead, and the dogs sitting around panting, all but two of the foxhounds and Gingersnap.

"Too late for the fracas," remarked Hilton, glancing at these last foxhounds. Then he proudly petted Dander. "Didn't need yer purp after all, ye see."

"Takes a heap of nerve for ten big dogs to face one little coyote," remarked the father, sarcastically. "Wait till we run onto a gray."

Next day we were out again, for I made up my mind to see it to a finish.

From a high point we caught sight of a moving speck of gray. A moving white speck stands for antelope, a red speck for fox, and a gray speck for either gray wolf or coyote—which of these is determined by its tail. If the glass shows the tail down it is a coyote; if up, it is the hated gray wolf.

Dander was shown the game as before and led the motley mixed procession—as he had before—greyhounds, wolfhounds, foxhounds, Danes, bull terrier, horsemen. We got a momentary view of the pursuit; a gray wolf it surely was, loping away ahead of the dogs. Somehow I thought the first dogs were not running as fast now as they had after the coyote. But no one knew the finish of the hunt. The dogs came back to us one by one, and we saw no more of that wolf.

Sarcastic remarks and recrimination were now freely indulged in by the hunters.

"Pah! scairt, plumb scairt," was the father's disgusted comment on the pack. "They could catch up easy enough, but when he turned on them, they lighted out for home—pah!"

"Where's that thar onsurpassable, fearless, scaired-o'-nort tarrier?" asked Hilton, scornfully.

"I don't know," said I. "I am inclined to think he never saw the wolf; but if he ever does, I'll bet he sails in for death or glory."

That night several cows were killed close to the ranch, and we were spurred on to another hunt.

It opened much like the last. Late in the afternoon we sighted a gray fellow with tail up, not half a mile off. Hilton called Dander up on the saddle. I acted on the idea and called Snap to mine. His legs were so short that he had to leap several times before he made it, scrambling up at last with my foot as a halfway station. I pointed and "sic-ed" for a minute before he saw the game, and then he started out after the greyhounds, already gone, with energy that was full of promise.

The chase this time led us not to the rough brakes along the river but toward the high open country, for reasons that appeared later. We were close together as we rose to the upland and sighted the chase half a mile off, just as Dander came up with the wolf and snapped at his haunch. The gray wolf turned around to fight, and we had a fine view. The dogs came up by twos and threes, barking at him in a ring; last, the little white one rushed up. He wasted no time barking, but rushed straight at the wolf's throat and missed it, yet seemed to get him by the nose; then the ten big dogs closed in, and in two minutes the wolf was dead. We had ridden hard to be in at the finish, and though our view was distant, we saw at least that Snap had lived up to the telegram as well as to my promises for him.

Now it was my turn to crow, and I did not lose the chance. Snap had shown them how, and at last the Mendoza pack had killed a gray wolf without help from the men.

There were two things to mar the victory somewhat; first, it was a young wolf, a mere cub, hence his foolish choice of country; second, Snap was wounded—the wolf had given him a bad cut in the shoulder.

As we rode in proud procession home, I saw he limped a little. "Here," I cried, "come up, Snap." He tried once or twice to jump to the saddle, but could not. "Here, Hilton, lift him up to me."

"Thanks; I'll let you handle your own rattlesnakes," was the reply, for all knew now that it was not safe to meddle with his person. "Here, Snap, take hold," I said, and held my quirt to him. He seized it, and by that I lifted him to the front of my saddle and so carried him home. I cared for him as though he had been a baby. He had shown those cattlemen how to fill the weak place in their pack; the foxhounds may be good and the greyhounds swift and the Russians and Danes fighters, but they are no use at all without the crowning moral force of grit, that none can supply so well as a bull terrier. On that day the cattlemen learned how to manage the wolf question, as you will find if ever you are at Mendoza; for every successful wolf pack there has with it a bull terrier, preferably of the Snap-Mendoza breed.

Next day was Hallowe'en, the anniversary of Snap's advent. The weather was clear, bright, not too cold, and there was no snow on the ground. The men usually celebrated the day with a hunt of some sort, and now, of course, wolves were the one object. To the disappointment of all, Snap was in bad shape with his wound. He slept, as usual, at my feet, and bloody stains now marked the place. He was not in condition to fight, but we were bound to have a wolf hunt, so he was beguiled to an outhouse and locked up, while we went off, I, at least, with a sense of impending disaster. I *knew* we should fail without my dog, but I did not realize how bad a failure it was to be.

Afar among the buttes of Skull Creek we had roamed when a white ball appeared bounding through the sagebrush, and in a minute more Snap came, growling and stump-waggling, up to my horse's side. I could not send him back; he would take no such orders, not even from me. His wound was looking bad, so I called him, held down the quirt, and jumped him to my saddle.

"There," I thought, "I'll keep you safe till we get home." Yes, I thought; but I reckoned not with Snap. The voice of Hilton, "Hu, hu," announced that he had sighted a wolf. Dander and Riley, his rival, both sprang to the point of observation, with the result that they collided and fell together, sprawling, in the sage. But Snap, gazing hard, had sighted the wolf not so very far off, and before I knew it he leaped from the saddle and bounded zigzag, high, low, in and under the sage, straight for the enemy, leading the whole pack for a few minutes. Not far, of course. The great greyhounds sighted the moving speck, and the usual procession strung out on the plain. It promised to be a fine hunt, for the wolf had less than half a mile start and all the dogs were fully interested.

"They've turned up Grizzly Gully," cried Garvin. "This way, and we can head them off."

So we turned and rode hard around the north side of Hulmer's Butte, while the chase seemed to go round the south.

We galloped to the top of Cedar Ridge and were about to ride down, when Hilton shouted, "By George, here he is! We're right onto him." He leaped from his horse, dropped the bridle, and ran forward. I did the same. A great gray wolf came lumbering across an open plain toward us. His head was low, his tail out level, and fifty yards behind him was Dander, sailing like a hawk over the ground, going twice as fast as the wolf. In a minute the hound was alongside and snapped, but bounded back as the wolf turned on him. They were just below us now and not fifty feet away. Garvin drew his revolver, but in a fateful moment Hilton interfered: "No; no; let's see it out." In a few seconds the next greyhound arrived, then the rest in order of swiftness. Each came up full of fight and fury, determined to go right in and tear the gray wolf to pieces; but each in turn swerved aside, and leaped and barked around at a safe distance. After a minute or so the Russians appeared—fine big dogs they were. Their distant intention no doubt was to dash right at the old wolf; but his fearless front, his sinewy frame and death-dealing jaws awed them long before they were near him, and they also joined the ring while the desperado in the middle faced this way and that, ready for any or all.

Now the Danes came up, huge-limbed creatures, any one of them as heavy as the wolf. I heard their heavy breathing tighten into a threatening sound as they plunged ahead, eager to tear the foe to pieces; but when they saw him there, grim, fearless, mighty of jaw, tireless of limb, ready to die if need be but sure of this, he would not die alone—well, those Great Danes—all three of them—were stricken as the rest had been with a sudden bashfulness: yes, they would go right in presently—not now, but as soon as they had got their breath; there were not afraid of a wolf, oh, no. I could read their courage in their voices. They knew perfectly well that the first dog to go in was going to get hurt, but never mind that— presently; they would bark a little more to get up enthusiasm.

And as the ten big dogs were leaping round the silent wolf at bay, there was a rustling in the sage at the far side of the place; then a snow-white rubber ball, it seemed, came bounding, but grew into a little bull terrier, and Snap, slowest of the pack, and last, came panting hard, so hard he seemed gasping.

Over the level open he made, straight to the changing ring around the cattle-killer whom none dared face. Did he hesitate? Not for an instant; through the ring of the yelping pack, straight for the old despot of the range, right for his throat he sprang; and the gray wolf struck with his twenty scimitars. But the little one, if foiled at all, sprang again, and then what came I hardly knew. There was a whirling mass of dogs. I thought I saw the little white one clinched on the gray wolf's nose. The pack was all around; we could not help them now. But they did not need us; they had a leader of dauntless mettle, and when in a little while the final scene was done, there on the ground lay the gray wolf, a giant of his kind, and clinched on his nose was the little white dog.

We were standing around within fifteen feet, ready to help, but had no chance till we were not needed.

The wolf was dead, and I hallooed to Snap, but he did not move. I bent over him. "Snap—Snap, it's all over; you've killed him." But the dog was very still, and now I saw two deep wounds in his body. I tried to lift him. "Let go, old fellow; it's all over." He growled feebly, and at last let go of the wolf. The rough cattlemen were kneeling around him now; old Penroof's voice was trembling as he muttered, "I wouldn't had him hurt for twenty steers." I lifted him in my arms, called to him and stroked his head. He snarled a little, a farewell as it proved, for he licked my hand as he did so, then never snarled again.

That was a sad ride home for me. There was the skin of a monstrous wolf, but no other hint of triumph. We buried the fearless one on a butte back of the ranch house. Penroof, as he stood by, was heard to grumble: "By jingo, that was grit—cl'ar grit! Ye can't raise cattle without grit."

He Did the Best He Could

FRED BAUER

One of our family's all-time favorite pets was a dog named Scampy. He was a black-and-tan, rag-eared mutt, part cocker, part Schnauzer, part whatcha-ma-call-it. When he was six months old, he was hit by a car and suffered a broken hind leg, which was put in a splint. Gangrene developed and the veterinarian recommended euthanasia. My children, however, full of love and affection for Scampy, lobbied for amputation and their tearful motion, put to a vote in a family council, was carried.

To my pleasant surprise, Scampy adjusted beautifully. Like a tricycle with the wheels reversed, he developed excellent balance and although running in unorthodox motion, he moved amazingly fast. Squirrels scattered when he flew off the back porch as though propelled by a pogo stick.

Friends of the children called him Hopalong or Tripod or Crip, among other names, but Scampy had a couple of advantages over people: He didn't understand their jibes and he didn't know that he was handicapped. He lived on courageously for many years, doing the best with what he had. People who can do the same are, I am convinced, the winners in life.

In Touch With God

"The first duty of love is to listen."

PAUL TILLICH

*I*f you feel closer to God when you're with his animals, you're not alone. Perhaps it's because they sense how we feel even when we can't put our feelings into words. Or, if we're ready to talk, they're ready to listen—with nothing but love in their eyes. Make a mistake and they won't hold it against you. They think you're pretty wonderful—just as God does.

Places of the Heart

TAIMUR MAHMOOD

$\mathcal{S}$ome places in the wild can rejuvenate the soul. These are places where you can heal emotional scars and old wounds by losing yourself in the beauty of the world. I have sought such places to rekindle my spirit and rediscover an innocence long forgotten. My journey is accompanied by three furry companions who have come to enlighten me on this odyssey of self-discovery. It is through them that I have found my passion for life.

In 1967 I immigrated to the United States from Pakistan with my American mother and our family of five after the death of our Pakistani father. I grew up in a dull, drab neighborhood outside of New Haven, Conn. My family was something of an oddity in a conservative New England town, where conformity was crucial to acceptance. I suffered a persistent melancholy for most of my adolescence because I was unable to "fit in."

Attending a prestigious prep school in my junior year of high school, I was unable to connect with anything or anybody. It was the lowest point in my life because I was immersed in a system of thought and conformity that seemed intolerable to me. I even contemplated killing myself. I lived with a low-grade, chronic depression never knowing what was missing in my world.

After finishing high school in 1978, I hitchhiked to Florida with a small suitcase and slept on the beach. I joined the ranks of the homeless and earned a scant income from temporary jobs and donating blood to plasma centers. It was my first exposure to raw humanity. I spent my days among prostitutes, junkies and fellow vagabonds, all seeking that elusive thing called "happiness."

Street life lost its appeal within a few weeks, so I took employment with the Sheraton Hotel in Fort Lauderdale and soon found my niche in the food and beverage industry. In the span of one year, I was a busboy, a room service waiter, a bartender and finally a manager. I used my experience to travel across America, working for many major hotel chains.

In the past, I always had searched for happiness in people, places and things that did not resonate with who I was. I had a family I could not turn to because I could not be what they wanted me to be. We held different values, and the things in life that seemed important to them were alien and distant to me. In many ways I was attempting to rekindle my sense of magic and awe that family life attempted to suffocate. This difference between us led to an odyssey of travel and adventure that changed my perception forever.

I discovered my love for photography when I began to explore the Colorado Rockies 20 years ago. There was a seclusion and silence on the mountaintops where my spirit found peace. From September 1982 through May 1988, I attended college in Boulder, Colo. Then I finally realized my real interest was exploring and capturing dynamic landscapes on film.

Disillusioned with campus life, I decided to embark on a 4,000-mile drive to Alaska in 1989. It was a revelation as I went into a wilderness of awe-inspiring mountains. This became an annual pilgrimage for me over the next seven years as I spent the summers in Anchorage working in a fine dining restaurant for an excellent income and the winters working in Vail, Colo.

In 1991, my second summer in Alaska, I met my first Labrador Retriever, Bandit. The 8-week-old was wrapped around a tree on a tiny leash and desperately needed a bath. His owner, a truck driver who was gone all day and who wrapped Bandit's mouth with duct tape when he got home so the puppy would not chew his shoes, gave me permission to take him on my daily photo excursions in the backcountry. Within a week, Bandit was mine.

It was a love affair of the most profound kind as this dog filled a void in my soul that I had long forgotten. Bandit's exuberance, zest for life and boundless energy were contagious. He was a "present moment" creature who seized every day with rapture and wonderment. I felt a great healing occurring within me. I grinned at his daily growth and felt like a millionaire being able to spoil him in the Alaskan wild.

In February of the following winter in Vail, Bandit and I were hiking in a wooded region across from the humane society. We encountered the volunteers taking the shelter dogs on their daily walk when Bandit saw his mirror image. His markings were identical to Bandit's, and his name was Barney. They licked and kissed each other like long-lost pals. I knew immediately these two would become lifelong friends. I called my patient, dog-loving girlfriend, Jebbie, and persuaded her to come see Barney. Within hours, he was mine. Bandit and Barney accompanied me everywhere as I drove through thousands of miles of national parks and backcountry.

Upon returning to Alaska in 1993, I found a roommate who had two (sometimes three) other dogs. I was delighted to see how Bandit and Barney got along with Nugget, a yellow Lab; Rip, a German Shepherd Dog; and Sarah, a Collie mix. Amazingly they all fit in my car, and off we went to trek the Alaskan countryside together.

On Valentine's Day of 1998 I got my third dog (Sassy) from the humane society. She was quite neurotic after having spent many months in confinement. Attention-starved and craving exercise, she slowly settled down once she, Bandit and Barney were able to explore the wilderness of the San Juan Mountains of southwestern Colorado, where I have spent the last two summers. The companionship of fellow Labs gave her a sense of security, and before long, she established herself in our home.

Dogs, just like humans, carry emotional scars from their pasts. The compassion, care and concern of their owners allow their spirits to rejuvenate and heal. Sassy was no different. Once she sensed her place was safe, she became self-assured and her personality transformed!

My life has been influenced deeply by these three dogs. I never knew I was a dog person, but something about their companionship is like a homecoming for me. Watching these creatures run as a pack is remarkable. They fill my days with joy and radiate pure enthusiasm on our excursions through the wild. Their capacity to love unconditionally and connect wholeheartedly has had a powerful influence on me. It has made me examine my beliefs and question what is real and meaningful in my life. I find that many of us are hypnotized by material wants and desires. We engross ourselves with stressful lifestyles that leave us empty and disillusioned. My dogs made me realize what is important.

The capacity to feel love daily and to engage myself in the

unfolding of the seasons is vital to my well-being. The dogs tune me in to a gentle and life-affirming frequency. As I watch them charge across Alpine snow fields playing tag, I get this ecstatic elation that I have found my place in the sun.

Often I am filled with a profound feeling of gratitude at being able to spend my days in the company of these creatures while pursuing my creative passion for photography in such extraordinary settings. My photography is a reflection of my inner search and venture toward self-understanding. It represents my need for creativity and clarity, and it has allowed me to explore a world of wonder in a time when things seem increasingly difficult to comprehend. These wild places suggest a higher order that gives me strength in confronting my daily challenges with patience and perseverance.

I continue to work in the hotel and resort industry to support my travels. Working as a waiter in fine dining establishments since 1978, I have lived in New England, Florida, West Virginia, Alaska, Hawaii, New Mexico and Colorado. I have been able to visit the Himalayas, Europe and Canada and use my photography to create nature segments for the Public Broadcasting Service choreographing my images to classical music. I also produce a stress-reduction video for the hospice community, and my programs have aired via satellite overseas by Heartland USA.

Our choices continually influence the quality of our lives. These dogs are extremely important to how I perceive my world. They act as a catalyst in my evolution, and through their company, I have come to sense my purpose in the world. They are constant reminders to me that we never should pretend to be something we are not. To delight in the simple joy of long walks, to cherish the feeling of the wind and to exercise and play daily are some of life's most important lessons.

I always have yearned for a sense of peace in my life. My dearest moments are in nature with my dogs by my side. It is in such landscapes that I am able to balance myself and visualize my humanity and connectedness to all things. These creatures add a dimension of love in my life that is hard to articulate. They are like Zen masters who live in the present moment—consciously and with tenderness. They are my greatest teachers, and as I discover my own joy, I can share this delight with the rest of the world.

from DOGWORLD

The Bird Feeder

SCOTT WALKER

$\mathcal{W}$hen we moved to Waco, Texas, my mother gave my family and me a housewarming present, something I *never* would have bought myself: a bird feeder.

I hung it from the limb of a magnolia tree outside our kitchen window. *A nice, decorative piece,* I thought. And for the first few days each morning, I looked out the window at the birds flocking to the feeder. But there was no food, so they came and went.

I need to fill their feeder with seed, I thought. So that afternoon I bought a twenty-pound sack of birdseed. Wouldn't you know? The warblers and the cardinals and the robins filled our yard with their color and song.

Mother's bird feeder was a rather odd present, but thank God for oddities. Because now I see the very wonderful effect it has had on my life as a point of daily spiritual focus. Feeding the birds reminds me that just as they are dependent on me for food and their lives are made that much easier, so am I dependent upon God in every aspect of my life.

A Little Kitten From Nowhere

SISSY BURGGRAF

The wisdom of an animal. How do you write about the ability of a creature that can have healthy young without pre-natal care; bear labor and delivery without someone sitting with them, and then raising those young without help of family or friends?

How do you write about a creature that will walk through fire, fight anyone or anything, no matter how large, to protect their family? Who will stay with you, love you, and protect you without question or conditions? How can you put that type of wisdom into words?

Shawn and I noticed immediately how very small she was the first time she walked into the racing stables where I worked as a groom.

We had no idea where she had come from, but we were amazed at how she had no fear of the massive race horses and would wrap her tiny body around their legs; entwining herself until her nose would touch her tail and she would look at us with those emerald eyes as if to ask, "so what are you staring at?"

The black kitten couldn't have been more than six months old and she was smaller than a southern minute. Mighty in character and soul, but oh so tiny! Such would earn her the name of "Termite."

Shawn, one of the horsemen, commented several times that he wished someone would take Termite home before she was kicked, or worse, stepped on, but no one offered the little kitten a home.

Later that afternoon, as one of the horsemen returned from jogging his horse on the track, the inevitable happened— Termite was kicked in the head as the horse came into the barn. Thrown across the aisleway, she was stunned but otherwise unhurt.

I was already the proud owner of twelve cats, and surely didn't need another, but on the other hand, thirteen WAS my lucky number! Termite would go home with me that evening.

Not only did I own twelve cats, three pet raccoons, and three horses, but I also had two dogs—Chentzy, a Doberman, and Ursula, my Great Dane.

Chentzy, Ursula and Termite would become steadfast friends immediately. Chentzy was twelve years old, losing her hearing to old age and her sight to cataracts. Termite would eat, sleep, and play with Chentzy and the two of them became inseparable. It wasn't long before Termite began to act as Chentzy's eyes and ears, Chentz relying on Termite for guidance everywhere they went.

Our house set well back from the road so Chentz was still permitted in the yard unsupervised. She and Termite would sunbathe in their favorite place and spend hours just napping together.

One afternoon I went outside to check on them and was horrified to find them gone! For more than an hour I searched, looking everywhere, but found no sign of them. As I stood quietly deciding my next step in finding them, I heard a faint, but desperate, meow. Looking around, I spotted Termite. She was coming from our neighbor's orchard!

I called for her and as she walked toward me, she kept looking over her shoulder at the orchard. Coming only to the edge of our property, I bent to pick her up and she ran from me, back to the direction from which she had come.

Three times she made the trip and three times she ran back. Finally, I decided to follow her. When we reached her destination, there lay Chentzy, unable to get up. Standing her on her feet and helping her to walk, we returned to the house with Termite in tow.

Only a few short weeks later, Chentzy had to be euthanized due to her continually failing health. She was laid to rest in one of her favorite places in the yard and for months, both Ursula and Termite would spend their hours lying on her grave.

The little kitten who had come from "nowhere" had proven to be a guardian angel to the least likely candidate—a Doberman. And now that her best friend was gone from her, she would continue to guard her grave.

Oliver's Shadow

LILLIAN ROBERTS

When the little beagle mysteriously showed up at our house one morning, I was quite upset. The last thing we needed was another dog. We already had a big German shepherd, Oliver North. Though good-natured, he could be a problem. Lots of deer forage through our rural setting and Oliver would break his chain in his anxiety to chase them. Often he'd be gone for hours at a time while my husband and I worried. Finally, he'd come loping home, winded and muddy from trying to keep up with animals far fleeter than he. I kept asking God to calm him down, but rambunctious pets didn't seem to be on his agenda.

On top of that, stress was coming in from all directions. My loving husband was beginning to show signs of Alzheimer's. And the bother of a strange dog was the last thing I needed. I tried to locate his owner in every way but to no avail. No one claimed him, which was easy to understand. Life hadn't been kind to the little fellow; he ambled with a limp and part of his tail was missing. So it seemed we were stuck with him.

Only Oliver seemed to tolerate him. I couldn't help but smile when I first saw the beagle climbing out of Oliver's dog house between the big shepherd's front legs. The only thing this odd couple had in common was their sable coloring.

Soon the beagle was straining my patience. More often

than not, after finishing his own bowl, he'd help himself to Oliver's. And those hamburger-sized paws! They soaked up mud like you wouldn't believe. The first time he stippled my freshly-mopped kitchen floor in crazy circles, I exploded in a fiery rage. And yet, as time went on, in some strange way, he began to have a calming effect on me. Maybe it was the "If you can't lick 'em, join 'em" syndrome. Perhaps it was the beagle's soulful brown eyes looking up at me so imploringly. But I found myself becoming more tolerant, relaxing instead of letting my blood pressure soar. And the eruptions were happening less and less. For example, instead of railing in exasperation when one or both would dig up my flower bed, I found it a simple matter to erect protective fencing.

And through it all God was answering my prayers about calming exuberant Oliver. More and more he seemed inclined to stay home to romp with his pal who we now called Shadow since the two were always together. There were still times, however, when Oliver strayed. How Shadow kept up with him we'll never know. Once, we were called to the back door by an unearthly yowling. There stood the beagle, looking up in dewy-eyed concern. He made it clear that we should follow him, so off we traipsed, Shadow eagerly limping ahead, tail stub waving, glancing back to make sure we were coming. Deep in the woods we found an "Oh-joy-to-see-you" Oliver, his broken collar chain entangled in the crevice of a fallen tree.

I was touched by the concern the smaller dog showed for his big friend. But a few months later something happened between the two which was unbelievable.

One day both Shadow and Oliver disappeared. A night passed, another, then three days, four. Frantic, I hesitated to leave the house in case the Humane Society called.

We spread the word everywhere, ran ads, distributed hand-bills, posted "Two Dogs Lost" notices. We called all the shelters around and I prayed, long and hard, that our dogs would return safely. After two weeks, a Humane Society staffer phoned us about finding a German shepherd. It wasn't Oliver, but I took the occasion to tell the man that "Whenever you find Oliver, you'll also find a little beagle."

There was a gulp on the other end.

"That your dog? Oh my, we have had those two here for almost two weeks," he explained excitedly. "Your shepherd had been hit by a car and when he was brought in, the little guy wouldn't leave his side. We tried to separate them but the beagle howled so loud we had to house them together.

"And you know what, Mrs. Roberts?" he continued. "You won't believe this, but that little fellow pulled that big dog from out of the middle of the road!"

"What . . . how?" I stammered.

"Wait 'til you see your big dog's ears. They're all chewed up. The driver that hit your dog insists he watched that little beagle drag that shepherd first by one ear, and then the other, pulling him to safety."

Sure enough, when we rescued Oliver, his ears were frayed. Outside of that, and a badly bruised hip, our vet pronounced him in good condition. The dogs, soon fully tagged, never ran away again.

Shadow's compassion was an inspiration to me. If a little dog could show that much loving concern for a hurt friend, I knew that, with God's help, I would have the patience and forbearance to be there for my loved one through the unknown year ahead.

Merry's Look Into the Future

HERB KUGEL

$\mathcal{C}$an dogs sense the future? Some believe a cocker spaniel named Merry could. In fact his fortune-telling ability saved the lives of his family.

The morning of June 30, 1944, marked the beginning of a beautiful day in Wimbledon, England, but the weather did little to lighten the lives of Mr. and Mrs. Baines and their 16-year-old daughter, Audrey. The Baines were living through the perilous times of World War II. Just one day earlier, a German V-1 rocket had landed one block from their home. Many were killed and maimed by the resulting explosion.

Despite the devastating attack, Merry, the family's silky, golden red cocker spaniel, was in his normal high spirits that morning as he trotted along with Mr. Baines down the front path of their home. However, Merry's stubby tail abruptly dropped as Mr. Baines, on his way to work, closed the front gate on him, locking him inside the yard.

Some time passed and Mrs. Baines and Audrey noticed that Merry was nowhere to be seen. This was unusual: the yard gates were latched and the high fence kept Merry from roaming. Mrs. Baines and Audrey looked everywhere for the dog but could find him nowhere. After searching the grounds, they carefully searched the entire house, then turned their attention back to the yard. This time Audrey noticed the plank guarding the opening to the underground bomb shelter had been knocked away.

The Baines had used the shelter frequently three years before, during the height of Germany's airborne assault on England. The shelter had always been a dank, morbid place, and as the German bombing raids declined, it fell into disrepair. Now the Baines and the rest of England faced a new airborne threat from the Germans' V-1 and V-2 rockets. However, the Baines preferred the shelter of a heavy steel table in the living room to the muggy, dark cellar.

A flashlight brought from the house revealed Merry happily curled up and asleep on the shelter's lowest bunk, the same bunk he had shared with Audrey during many air raids. Merry had not gone anywhere near the old shelter in years, because it was no longer used by the Baines, yet now he was comfortably sleeping in it despite the horrible smell and gloomy darkness. Audrey forced herself to ignore the stench and the green slime that covered the floor as she descended into the shelter and retrieved Merry. Once back in daylight, she carefully replaced the board covering the shelter entrance.

Three times that morning Audrey found the board knocked away and Merry asleep on the same bunk. Audrey and her mother could not understand Merry's behavior, yet after three trips into the shelter, they agreed the underground cellar was more secure than the underneath of any table. They began to clean the shelter. Surprisingly Merry's interest in the shelter abruptly vanished when he saw the Baines women begin the cleanup. His behavior reverted to normal, and he went cheerfully on about his daily adventures.

The Baines lived at the address of 10 Melbury Gardens. That night, with warnings of more rocket attacks, they were joined in their underground shelter by Mrs. Gearing, their neighbor at 14 Melbury Gardens who frequently took shelter with the Baines during air raids. At 2:50 a.m., when everyone in the shelter was asleep, a rocket exploded in front of the houses numbered 10 to 14 Melbury Gardens. The buildings were completely demolished. Had the Baines and Mrs. Gearing not gone into the underground shelter that night, it is certain they would have been injured or killed.

How did Merry sense the coming danger? How did he know that Mrs. Baines and Audrey would look for him in the unused shelter? The answer, of course, is unknowable, but one thing seems certain. The Baines and Mrs. Gearing would not have lived to tell the tale if Merry had not acted as he did.

from DOG & KENNEL

Out of the Nest

KATHRYN LAY

I knew something was going on when I heard the frantic chirping outside. My eight-year-old daughter and I ran around the side of the house and saw a beautiful pair of cardinals swooping around their baby sitting on the ground, peeping as loud as its tiny lungs allowed.

My daughter, who dearly loves all things great and small, squealed as a neighbor's dog bounded into our yard. We scrambled for the cardinal chick as the neighbor kids tugged at their dog's leash. Soon the baby bird was safe in a basket. We quickly began searching for the cardinal nest as parents and chick cried out to one another.

A loud roar and our neighbor was mowing the yard, right over the area where the chick had been. "We rescued the baby," my daughter said. Once again I had become a hero in her eyes, the second time to save a baby bird in a year. I was proud, yet I ached for the worried parents.

We made phone calls to local wildlife refuges, bird rehabilitators, and veterinarians. They encouraged us to put the bird into a basket and into a tree to let the parents care for it. I searched my collection of baskets for the tallest one, transferred the cheeping bird, and watched as my husband wedged it into the fork of the tree where the parents sat, waiting and watching.

Within seconds the feathered baby bird was sitting on the edge of the basket. He leapt earthward, his tiny wings fluttering long enough to settle into the middle of the road. Another frantic scramble and we had the bird again. I looked into its tiny, peeping face and wondered why the creature felt compelled to wander from the nest when he obviously wasn't ready to fly the distance. Why did that baby bird insist on independence over parental watchfulness?

Thunderstorms were predicted for the night and Cheep-Cheep found a home in my office. The next morning, I called a wildlife store. The manager explained that we should return it outside for the parents to care for on the ground. If we tried to raise it, the bird would probably die when we set it free. It needed guidance from its parents who would teach the bird to find food, water, and shelter. "They even teach him how to waterproof his feathers," he explained.

My daughter wept as we set it free. Within moments, the parents arrived. We watched in fascination as the mother cardinal swooped down to the chick, then flew away. Over and over she came and went, always leaving in the same direction. The baby followed as best it could. Finally, it stopped to rest in the grassy shade of a tree.

Mom and Dad Cardinal never left their post in that tree, coming down to feed their baby occasionally. A loud raucous sound brought us outside again to see a desperate fight between Daddy Cardinal and a large bluejay. We marveled at the way the parents protected and cared for the lost bird, unwilling to abandon it.

Hours later, they were gone. We did not know what hap-

pened. We only hoped the baby was able to take wing and follow its parents to a safer place.

Many of my friends' children are at the ages where they are
leaping from the nest. Learning to drive. Finding their own
apartments. Heading off to college. Preparing for marriage. I
watch as my friends try to hold on, yet letting go because they
know they must, even as fears for their children's safety attack
their thoughts like invading bluejays.

I watch my daughter, always independent, always ready to
take a new risk. Each age seems to bring new chances for her
to slip away from the nest. School trips, visits with friends,
times when I must depend on the knowledge and care of
others for her safety. I find it hard to let go. Instead, I want to
build the walls of the nest higher so that she can't leap over the
edge. And yet, I work at preparing her to face that independent
future, helping her to know how to care for herself. Her father
is fiercely protective, and I know how difficult it will be to
watch her take her first real flight as he scours the world
around her for big dogs, bluejays, and other dangers along
the way.

The wild bird store owner explained that the babies often
leap from the nest several days before they are truly ready to
fly. The parents are watchful, caring for the chick as needed
until it is fully independent. I scour books and articles and talk
with friends who have older children as I search for answers to
my heart's fears about my daughter.

But it was my experience with this cardinal family that gave
me peace to know that as my chick flies farther and farther
away, I can still reach out to her when she needs me, and trust
that my teachings will prepare her for life away from the nest.

"Don't worry, Mom," she encourages as I drop her off to a

waiting bus for a field trip. "I'll be careful, Mom," she promises when she leaves to spend the night with a friend. It is Mom who isn't ready to let go, tempted to clip her baby's developing wings.

Several days after we set the baby cardinal free, Michelle was sure she saw it fly over the rooftop. I have often seen the parents in our backyard. They aren't frantically searching any longer. Their songs aren't filled with anxiety, but joy.

Although my heart beats faster and my hands clench, I watch my daughter find her independence, and search for my own song.

Herman, a Special Gift

NICOLE CAUGHLIN

I tell everyone that my cat, Herman, is a special gift from God. I cannot imagine life after him, nor can I figure out how I lived before him. In this world, where change is the only constant, Herman has been an unwavering friend.

He found me quite by accident, actually. My husband and I were going to visit a friend of his out on a farm. I love farms, having grown up in rural Wisconsin, and the prospect of a trip to one set my homesick heart aflutter.

When we pulled into the driveway, the first thing I saw was a rangy yellow cat standing on the hood of a car. He had the oddest face, one that looked disproportionate in some unidentifiable way. I love cats, so I was immediately drawn to him. His name was Boots, in reference to his white-stockinged feet. While my husband and his friend discussed engines and carburetors, I bonded with Boots. I was sad when it was time to leave, but I knew we'd see Boots again.

I got into the car and patiently waited for my husband to finish his conversation. Suddenly, the door to the car flew open and my husband said, "Do you want a cat?" Did I ever!

Suddenly the charming little cat was vaulted into my lap and the door was slammed. Apparently Boots was a leftover of a failed relationship and was not wanted. I was glad to take him because my husband and I were newly married and did not have any pets yet. Thus was the beginning of a beautiful friendship. . . .

I looked at Boots and really didn't think the name fit him . . . he was much more unique than "Boots." I thought of my uncle who used to take me fishing as a child, and decided on the name Herman. Herman approved, and it is the only name he has ever responded to. If you call him Boots he just gives you a dirty look.

Unfortunately, Herman was emaciated and I feared that he might be sick. So we took him to the vet first thing in the morning. And there was bad news: Herman had FIV, which is the feline equivalent to AIDS. Apparently this disease is very common to outdoor cats, especially males. I was heartbroken. The vet told me that he might not live very long and that I should have him put to sleep. I couldn't do it. Now, I am no shrinking violet here. I worked in a vet clinic the prior summer and I have doctored up stray animals my entire life. But there was something about Herman that made me think he could manage despite the disease. And he did.

"Hermie," as we came to call him, was eight pounds soaking wet. Well, no animal of mine was going to go around skinny like that! We fed him high-quality food and nice fresh water, and he blossomed into an astounding 20-pound tabby. Yes, a tabby! When his old fur began to shed, a beautiful orange tabby coat came in.

Herman is now the absolute picture of feline health. We have had him for four years, and I have never regretted the decision to stick with him. Granted, he has had some minor illnesses related to the FIV. His gums become inflamed so he needs occasional courses of interferon treatments, and he keeps getting these pesky eye infections. I am prepared in my heart for the possibility that one day he will be truly ill. But I trust that God will continue to take care of him as well as He has.

So, you may ask, what is so astounding about this cat? Well, besides his unswerving love and loyalty, he is the most intelligent animal I have ever known. And I have known many animals! Hermie has invented his own games, learned to open doors and cabinets, and has taught me to speak fluent "feline." The game he invented is called "There It Goes." Basically, it is fetch with a Q-Tip, but you have to shout "There it goes!" otherwise he will not bring it back. It is impossible to hide anything from him, too. He has learned to negotiate doors and kiddie cabinet locks. Herman also washes his food before eating, and throws water at people he doesn't like.

But the most amazing thing about Herman is his compassion. He has shown me unconditional love unlike any human. It is because of him that I truly began to understand the love Christ has for me. And that's how I know he was a special gift from the Lord. If I cry, he strokes my cheek with his paw. If I am cold, he will lie on my feet. He always seems to know what I need. He is my constant companion from morning to evening. When I awake he is there to greet me. If I cannot sleep, he keeps me company. When I eat breakfast, he sits in the chair beside me and talks about his day. He never yells, he never interrupts, and he never hurts me. I thank the Lord for him every moment of every day. Herman has shown me God's unconditional love.

Something Magical

SUSAN CHERNAK McELROY

$\mathcal{I}$ was surprised to find myself so smitten with Phaedra. I've never been especially enchanted with llamas, probably because I had been spit upon by so many when I once worked for a baby zoo. When I first saw Phaedra, she was standing in a field of daisies, her fluffy white coat dusted with dried flowers and bits of grass. She looked like a tiny fairy, big-eyed, delicate, and graceful as a deer on her tapered white legs. She was much smaller than any of the other llamas in the field and I mistook her for a baby until her owner told me that something had gone awry in her growth centers and she was dwarfed. To me, her babyish look only added to her unique appeal. Something about her seemed almost magical. Phaedra had a serene and delicate gentleness about her I'd never seen in a llama, and my heart was instantly and hopelessly lost to her.

At the time, Lee and I were fantasizing that Brightstar could be a going business concern and we could possibly raise certain stock animals for profit. We had selected miniature donkeys for our business venture, not because they made phenomenally good business sense, but because we loved them and, frankly, I wanted a good excuse to have more of them around. As luck would have it, the donkeys would indeed make stable business partners. Profits from selling their babies, though nothing to break the bank, would go a long way toward keeping all the other animals on the farm fed and cared for. Meanwhile, our small core herd of five would provide us with wonderful fertilizer, yard-trimming services, and their incomparable old-soul donkey presence.

Llamas, however, were not in our business plan. Their market had gone "soft." So when Phaedra walked up to me and nuzzled my cheek with a nose as soft as feathers, I bit my lip and turned away toward the other pasture—the one that held the miniature donkeys. Although I left Phaedra standing in the field that day, my heart was with her constantly. I made excuses to go back to the farm where she lived just to see her again. As the months went by, I noticed that Phaedra was getting a bit thinner, and that her coat had less sheen to it than I had remembered, but I didn't think much about it. Our farm was busy with babies, and my concerns were for my animal family at home.

I didn't see Phaedra again for nearly a year, but late in the fall I managed to visit her. As she walked across the pasture to greet me, I could hardly believe that this was the same animal I'd seen the year before. Her coat was caked with mud and burrs and was a dull, lifeless gray. Blackflies swarmed at the thick yellow discharge around her eyes and feasted on her filthy ears until they drew blood. When I rested my hands on her back, rib and bone moved beneath my fingers. She was a skeleton.

Size and deformity had betrayed her. As the other llamas in the pasture had grown tall and powerful, Phaedra was no match for them at the hay and grain bins. Too small to compete for food, she waited and she starved. She became the object of the herd's abuse, as weakened animals often are, and was a special target of the herdsire, who would knock her off her feet to breed. The stud had struck her down endlessly, coming at her like a log battering ram, eventually breaking her small face and jaw. Afterward, Phaedra learned to stay on the ground most of the day, to avoid the attention of the stud. Then another complication set in. Phaedra's eyesight was failing, perhaps because of her injuries. She had no night vision and spotty vision at best during the day. A night-light burned in her barn, and she would sleep beneath it, unsteady on her feet if she left the circle of dim yellow light. All this was told to me by the young man who owned her. He was a kind and loving man, the situation with Phaedra being one of those tragic things that sometimes happens on a farm, with many, many animals all needing time, care, and attention. He had moved Phaedra away from the herd to her own small pasture, but still, she continued to fail.

From the moment I first saw Phaedra, I knew she belonged with me. Yet even in the midst of her terrible suffering, I didn't ask to bring her home. I tried to stay within the limits Lee and I had set for our farm. Our animal family was enormous. Our financial resources were limited. There was no money left for new animals. In tears, I told myself to be an adult while my heart cracked inside of me. I remembered the words I said to myself when I worked for a humane society and euthanized animals every day: "Susan, you can't save them all. You can't."

And so I returned home and Phaedra stayed in her pasture. Early next spring, I went to see her again. She had made it through winter, but she looked worse. Her owner told me that earlier that week, she had fallen and couldn't get to her feet without help. She was a filthy, bony bundle of health problems and vet bills, and I heard myself say, "Please let me take her home." The next thing I knew, she was in the back of my van, kneeling quietly on a cushion of straw as we drove home to Brightstar. I imagined that Lee would have fits when I got there. Of course he didn't.

Phaedra stumbled out of the van and into our pastures, a frail, unsteady creature with an uncertain future. She took a few hesitant steps toward our barn and stopped a moment to sniff the branch of an apple tree. Her lips pursed into a Betty Boop pucker, and she uttered a questioning sort of murmur and looked back at me. The heart performs miracles: I saw a dainty, glittering fairy blessing our pastures with beauty and tranquility, where anyone else would have seen a ball of dirt on stick legs.

Phaedra became my summer project. Each day I sang songs to her about fairies while I washed the dirt and fly crusts off of her ears and eyes and worked the burrs out of her fur. I treated her sore, swollen eyes with drops and wiped bug repellent on her face and ears. One day I got industrious and cut off her matted hair with a pair of scissors. My hands blistered and my wrists ached for days, but the results were worth it. Beneath the old dead coat was a fine white blanket of soft fur. My hope was that love, good food, and good care would be enough to bring Phaedra back to health, but fate fought me at every turn. First, it was a bad abscess in her cheek, near her once-broken jaw. Then it was diarrhea brought on by the antibiotics to fight the abscess. Next she quit eating. Finally she developed an ulcer. I poured Maalox down her throat three times a day, marveling that she didn't spit it back at me. In time, I realized that Phaedra could no longer chew hay or grass, and that grain passed through her unchewed and indigested. I put her on a special pelleted formula. She turned her nose up at three different brands, then finally accepted the fourth. The vet became such a regular visitor that I joked with him about setting up a cot in our barn.

Weeks passed and I asked myself—as Lee often asked—what on earth was I doing. There were countless other projects, other tasks that needed my time and attention. Yet I let them fall by the wayside, focusing my energy on Phaedra, my precious, gentle fairy. For reasons I could never hope to explain to anyone, myself included, Phaedra simply enchanted me. I would find myself spending hours just watching her walk around the pasture or sprawl luxuriously in the sun. Sometimes she would gaze up at a flock of birds overhead or sniff at the bees on a cluster of clover. One day, in the soft breeze of a late summer afternoon, I saw her leap around the pasture like a gazelle, all four legs straight beneath her, springing high up into the air as she tossed her head left and right in rapturous abandon. It is my most precious memory of her.

Despite all my loving care, Phaedra failed to thrive. She lived in a state of frail health, not gaining much ground, occasionally losing some. Her vet and food bills were hitting the catastrophic mark when I told Lee, out of shame for my lack of more mature and logical behavior, that I wouldn't spend any more money on her, that I would put her to sleep before she ran up any more big bills. Lee saw the pain in my eyes and, trying to spare me and our shrinking wallet, said, "No more charity cases, okay?" I turned away and muttered, "Yes, okay."

For the next few days, those words echoed in my head: *no more charity cases.* I've learned to listen carefully when my inner buzzer goes off, as it was doing, because it usually means that I'm about to learn something of importance, if I listen closely and keep my mind and heart wide open.

One evening later that week, I sat in the barn with Phaedra and watched as she ate one or two pellets at a time. I asked her out loud the questions I had only asked myself. I asked her what she was doing at our farm, why she had called so strongly to me, and what she needed to teach me. Sitting on a bucket beside her, I closed my eyes and reached out my arms to her, waiting for whatever thoughts might come to me.

No more charity cases. Visions of a lifetime of hurt and lost animals drifted up before me. I had taken them all home—dogs, kittens, birds, half-squashed toads—and spent my last dime on them. I loved them, found them new homes, sometimes healed them, too often buried them. I remembered telling Lee before we were married that sometimes my affinity for animals wouldn't seem so cute. It would involve stopping in the middle of the road to carry a snake to a curb when we were already late for a party. Or it might involve a bathtub full of some sick creature that honks or cries all night. It would be money and emotion and tears spent on some broken, lost sick being. "You will get sick of it, and sick of me," I told him. He had not, or if so, only fleetingly. *I* was getting sick of it, sorry for it, ashamed of it. *Ashamed of it.* It's only an animal. Are all llamas that ugly? Why don't you put your energy into *people* charities? It seemed I had spent a lifetime explaining, justifying, apologizing. Even with a book about the virtues of animals to my credit, I still felt shame.

Could I have chosen my passion, I would not have chosen animals. In my desperate need to be liked, I would have selected a more politically correct cause on which to spend my life's passion. But I did not *choose, I was chosen.* Chosen long before I could even talk. My first words were about animals; my first joys, my first death, and my first births involved animals. When I was stricken with cancer in my late thirties, it was a lifetime of experience with animals living and dying in my home and in my arms that offered me a vision of healing. In a very real sense, animals had given me my life.

I heard Phaedra finish the last of her pellets. In the outstretched circle of my arms, she settled down on her knees and began working her cud. I stayed very still and continued to listen. Phaedra, for all the effort of her care, had brought me so many good things. In the hours I had spent with her, she had brought me back to a sense of childlike mystery. With Phaedra in the pasture, I could believe in fairies again. I could stop and take time to sit and daydream. Her gentle nature calmed me and brought me many moments of quiet and thanksgiving. She shared with me her joy and steadfast companionship. For what I had given her, she had given me back tenfold. *Tenfold.* This is how I tithe. My eyes flew open and met the quiet brown sea of Phaedra's kindly gaze. Her face was soft, her eyes clear and bottomless. The banana ears she swiveled toward me were white and clean. She leaned into me and gently sniffed my face. When I rubbed her neck, I realized that her bones were beginning to disappear behind a new layer of muscle. There had been improvements, albeit small ones. She would be fine. We would be fine. Shame melted for the time being. I knew it would return, but each time I would feel the sting of it less and less. This is how I tithe, not with money or checks but with time and love willingly given to a decades-long chain of animals who found their way to me, who chose me, healed me, empowered me: the charity cases. God grant me a never-ending stream of charity cases. When I left the barn that night and returned to the house, it was to tell Lee that I would be cutting off my very arms and legs if there were no place at our farm for charity cases. And of course he understood. It was I who needed to understand, and it was Phaedra who had chosen to teach me.

from ANIMALS AS GUIDES FOR THE SOUL

LESSONS IN LIVING

"If you can bond with an animal,
you can understand how
human beings work."

MICHELLE JAMES

*I*n springtime, in the rural area where I live, the air is filled with the sounds of birds—calling to each other, carrying twigs and grasses to build their nests, fighting off intruders, hatching their eggs and teaching their youngsters how to survive. Then, when the weather changes, they leave to do the same thing somewhere else. But it's comforting to know that they'll be back and that they'll go on with their lives. They remind us that life itself is a great blessing.

Homer and Ann

RICK BASS

All of my dogs have been wonderful accidents that have happened to me and now I am drowning in dogs and it is wonderful. I go to sleep amid the sounds of dogs stirring, settling in for the night downstairs, and wake up in the early morning to their whimpers and yawns and stretches. Of the first two dogs I ever owned as an adult, one, Homer, is still with me after fifteen years. Homer and Ann were black and tan Mississippi hounds of some unpatented beagle and walker hound and black and tan mix. When I found them, they were mangy and worm-ridden, and I only meant to take them to the animal shelter.

I was driving down a back road in Mississippi at dusk when I saw two tiny pups, one slender, one heavy, sitting by the roadside next to a third pup lying dead in the road. The slender pup, wild as the wind, galloped up a narrow game trail, arched with thorns and brambles of blackberry bushes, leapt up onto the splintered porch of an old abandoned house, and darted through an open door, disappearing into the dark maw of ruin.

I followed cautiously. I searched each room, half-fearing that humans, under the most dire of straits, might still be camping in that rubble, but each room was empty. When I came to the back porch, I saw that it opened out into the exuberant jungle of Mississippi in June. (The pups appeared to have just been weaned, seven weeks, which would place their birth sometime around Easter.)

I marveled at the slender pup's speed and wildness, imagining what it must have been like for that little wild thing to leap from the back porch down into that brambly thicket. A little sadly, I turned and went back to my truck, to the other pup still waiting by the roadside.

No matter, I told myself; a pup wild as that slender one—more of a coyote, really—wouldn't have made a very good pet anyway.

I got in the truck with the heavy pup, who wagged her tail and blinked her long eyelashes at me, ecstatic, and I drove on down the road.

With what subtle assuagements does landscape sculpt our hearts, our emotions; and from that catalyst, sometimes, our actions? I followed the winding road through the dusk tunnel of soft green light, and as I passed by the same place, a couple hundred yards down the road, where I'd first felt the impulse to turn around and go back for the pups, I felt it again. It was a feeling, a change, as dramatic as if I had passed through a doorway, and into an entirely different room. *You know,* I thought, *I ought not to split those little pups up like that.*

I turned around at about the same spot in the road and went back to give it one more try.

When I pulled back up to the abandoned house, the slender pup, Homer, was sitting out on the side of the road, in the same place where she had been earlier. I stopped the truck and jumped out, at which point she whirled and bolted, scampered up the viney trail and right back into the dark old falling-down house. I hurried after her, and once more went from room to room, looking for a tiny frightened wild pup, but found nothing, only decay. And once more I came finally to the back porch, with its storm-sprung doorless frame yawing straight into the gloom of jungle beyond.

What a pup, I marveled. *What a wild thing, making that four-foot leap into thorn and bramble. Too wild,* I thought again sadly, though my sorrow was tempered by the pleasure of having salvaged the one sweet little pup, and I returned to the truck knowing somehow that she would make a wonderful pet for someone; and, as before, she was thrilled to see me: thrilled to be petted, belly-thumped, noticed. Not yet loved, but noticed.

It was just before dark. I drove on down the road; and, amazingly, as I passed through that same invisible curtain— a curve of landscape, a mosaic of forest, and an open field beyond—I had the same feeling I'd had both times before. *There's still just a* little *bit of light left; I ought to try one more time. I ought to use up that last little bit of light trying.*

I turned around and went back to the old house. And again, the little hound was perched out front, roadside.

This time when she saw my truck she whirled and ran for the house even before I'd stopped; but I was quick, this time, and leapt from my truck and crossed the road in long strides, and hurdled the sagging, rusted iron gate, and plowed through the brambles, gaining on the pup.

She scampered up the steps and into the house. I was close behind, and this time I went straight to the back, hoping to catch her before she made that amazing leap.

But not quite. I was just a little too late, for when I came to that blasted-out doorway, again there was nothing but space, emptiness, and jungle beyond. The evening's first fireflies were beginning to cruise, as if sealing over the space into which the little hound had leapt, in the same manner with which the rings on a pond settle out to flatness, sealing over a stone that has been tossed into the pond's center.

Foiled again, and feeling a little foolish, a little defeated, and anxious to get on over to Elizabeth's before it got to be too late, I turned to go back to my truck, and to the one waiting puppy, again.

I was halfway down the hallway—the disintegrating shack eerie, ominous, in the failing light—when a new thought occurred to me: as if it had taken a shift in lighting to shove away an old assumption, and yield—tentatively, cautiously, at first— a new perspective.

That back-porch leap would be a heck of a jump for an animal as small as that pup to make; and to be making it again and again, so *relentlessly:* well, wasn't that a bit much? And how was she getting all the way out to the front of the house again so quickly, each time, after being swallowed by the jungle?

In all my previous explorations, I'd only glanced in each room. There was only the dullest blue light remaining, here and there, in the house. Dusk's first stars visible through the cracks and rips in the roof. Owls calling.

I went from room to room, checking behind the old moldering cardboard boxes of pots and pans, and rotting clothes, and mildewed ancient magazines, fast on their way to becoming humus. In each room, nothing, until I got to the last room—a wild clutter of yellowing newspapers—where I noticed what I had not before, a littering of small, dried-out twists of dog dung. As if they had been living in this room for quite some time.

There was a pile of loose sheets of newspaper over in the

far corner of the room, by the window, and in the dim light, I could see that the papers were rattling slightly, as if from a breeze. I stepped over to the corner and lifted the sheets of paper, and there she was, tinier than I had remembered, and no longer fierce or barksome, and no longer any super dog, capable of great and daring leaps of escape, but instead a quivering, terrified little pup.

She was warm when I picked her up, and this time she did not resist. I tucked her in against my body and carried her out into the night to rejoin her sister.

Cows were lowing in the fields, a summer sound, when I arrived at Elizabeth's farmhouse. Steam was drifting in from off of the bayou.

"What are you going to do with them?" Elizabeth asked.

"Oh, I'll take them to the animal rescue league tomorrow," I said—never dreaming or imagining otherwise—though a short time later, as we watched them crouch bowlegged in front of a pan of milk and gulp at it until their bellies were stretched thumping tight, their tails wagging, it must have occurred to me, just the faintest shadow of a thought at first, *Well, I guess I could wait a day or two . . .*

Homer was named for the orphan Homer Wells, in John Irving's novel *The Cider House Rules,* which I was reading at the time. There was something about her slender elegance, even in her temporary disarray—patchy fur, burrs, etc.—that told me she was feminine enough to carry such a name, and to turn it from the masculine to the feminine.

Ann was named for Orphan Annie.

They slept in a cardboard box together—under a thin sheet, their heads tucked against each other's shoulders. They slept soundly, not whining at all the way most pups do, but snoring slightly—as if completely content, now that they had finally gotten to where they needed to be. Having given them a little milk, and assigned them names, how could I turn them away?

I held them tiny in my hands. I followed them as if through a door, and nothing was ever the same. By stopping four, five minutes and picking up those sweet, funny, vulnerable little hounds, I stepped off the train tracks of my old life and into a slightly different world, where I stood at peace at the edge of shadows and sun dapple.

When we moved to Montana the dogs were depressed at first, missing Mississippi; they lay by the back door of the cabin for a solid month. But they grew accustomed to the new country and fell in love with life again. They went for hikes with me, chased the coyotes out of the yard, learned the new scents, new routines. They became mountain dogs soon enough; they refashioned themselves, out of loyalty. They learned about snow, about the values of a spot by the fireplace on a cold evening and the glories of muddy spring. They learned how certain things were backwards here, such as the geese leaving in the autumn, rather than arriving.

What else was there to do but adjust, and to love life?

I would often observe their loyalty, and watch their pleasure in this new place in the world, and try, in some units of measurement not yet known to man, to quantify the distance they had come, from being at death's door in Mississippi to chewing on a moldering old elk skull outside the cabin in Montana.

And I realized, soon enough, that that distance for them was the same distance for me.

from COLTER

The Ultimate Couch Pigtato

CYNNDE NIELSEN AND ED KOSTRO

Miss Belle, the Vietnamese potbellied pig, arrived at Misty Hollow Farm about a year ago. Practically a newborn, she was so small, cuddly, and defenseless, her new owners allowed her access to the family home, never realizing how resourceful she really was.

She studied the behavior of the house felines. She would follow them around, play with them, take naps with them, and even use their litter boxes. She was definitely a quick study. She was soon rewarded with fruit treats and jelly beans for her fine efforts.

As Belle grew, she began studying the dogs who were allowed to wander in and out of the house in an enclosed area, to romp and play in the yard, and to sleep on cozy rugs in the den. They were also house-trained. Belle began to heed the call of nature outside, for which she was rewarded with pieces of cheese and more jelly beans.

As she dozed off on a nice plush rug one night, she decided that it was time to begin her final semester of study: observing her human owners. She soon discovered they ate three meals a day, every day. Since Miss Belle now weighed in at 75 pounds, her appetite and her desire for the better things in life were growing fast. She too began receiving three meals a day. She was given cereal and fruit in the morning, granola bars and fruit juices for lunch, and salad greens and piggy kibble for dinner. Life was indeed good, and it was getting better every minute.

She still had homework to do. Crafty Miss Belle began to study and follow every move of these humans long after dinner.

On a typical evening at the farm, the humans can be found sprawled out on their favorite recliners in the family room, watching a movie, reading, dozing, or munching on snacks. Beside them on the nice, warm, comfortable sofa, you will also now find a rather unique "couch potato"—none other than rotund, happy, shrewd Miss Belle. She has even convinced her friend and constant companion, Taylor the cat, to occasionally join her on this extremely comfortable piece of furniture. On many an evening, you can now find old Taylor snuggled up next to, or even on top of, Miss Belle, as the two cat-nap and pig-nap the evening away.

from PETS: PART OF THE FAMILY

Return of the Ducks

ARDITH CLARKE

Lorraine, her coat buttoned askew and her hat on backwards, was struggling into her new red boots.

"Where do you think you're going?" I asked.

"To the pond—to see if the ducks are back yet," she said.

"We can see from here that they aren't. I don't think they are coming back, ever." She looked at me, her eyes wide with disbelief. I tried to soften my words. "I'm sure they've found another home by now. It must be a good one or they would not have stayed."

She was too young to be burdened with facts about the helplessness of wild ducks whose wings have been clipped. The two ducks we named Mr. Drake and Mrs. Hen had been extras in an experimental program from my husband's work. He had brought them home hoping to shelter and feed them until fall when they could forage for themselves and their feathers would be long enough for flight. Each morning he had carried them to a pen he had made for them at our pond and each night he had brought them in again.

One night the pen had been empty. Coyotes? Hunters? A half-starved dog we had seen loping across the field? The red-winged hawk that patrolled our meadow? We speculated about what had devoured our ducks. We knew they were dead, but we told Lorraine only that they were gone.

"I hope they aren't wet." She had abandoned the boot project and was peering out the window, nose flattened against the pane.

"If they are out in this, they are wet. The whole world is wet—dripping, oozing wet." Fog and mist had blanketed our world for days, hiding any glimmer of sunlight. Suddenly I felt very sorry for myself. Despair, like the mist, had blanketed my husband and myself for so long that there was little happiness left for us. No matter where I sent my thoughts, they could not penetrate the gloom engulfing me. The doctor had told us that because of complications in early pregnancy there was a chance our coming baby would be deformed.

"Will it have a defective mind or just a twisted little toe?" I had asked.

"No way to tell what the deformity is or even if there is one," the doctor had said. "All I can tell you is the statistic in a case like this—one-out-of-five chance for deformity."

And so the statistic had become my ghostly companion, enfolding me like thick fog, seeping into my brain until not one part of my present or future was free of a feeling of impending disaster.

I sat down at the table with a cup of steaming tea and gazed out the window upon the barren fields of late fall, trying not to think. The pond that had teemed in the summer heat with ripples and sunshine lay bleak and lifeless in the clutches of approaching winter. The brown pool was as still as the barren fields beyond.

Then a shadow moved against the bank and a ripple of life streaked across the water. I grabbed the binoculars from the desk and focused. Mr. Drake—our Mr. Drake—his green head erect, glided elegantly across the water, at ease, at home, as though he had never been gone. Mrs. Hen, her soft brown body almost indistinguishable from the muddy bank and water, was right beside him.

"The ducks are back!" I shouted. "Get into your coat and boots. The ducks are back." I forgot my stuffy nose, my ballooning stomach and statistics. All I could think about was serving the ducks a good-sized meal before they decided to go.

As I filled their pen with cracked grain, the ducks waddled up the far bank, loudly scolding my interruption. And as I watched their clumsy retreat, I marveled that two fat, grounded mallards could strut around the countryside for 10 days without being eaten or run over. What had been their chances of survival? One chance out of 50? One out of 100? And if they did survive, what had been the chances of their returning to our little pond? One chance out of 100? One out of 1000? Whatever the odds, I'm sure the statistics were against the ducks, but they had survived the statistics; they had returned.

"I knew they'd be back. I knew they'd be back," Lorraine chanted, hopping on one foot and then the other. I smiled at her, knowing how easy it had been for her to believe in the ducks' return. She had not known the obstacles. She had never been filled with doubts.

Then, as always, my thoughts plunged inward again, but this time with different emphasis. I thought of my baby's statistics, my fears and apprehensions. Oh God, I had dwelt on the one out of five chances for abnormalcy. Why had I lived in despair these past few months when I could have lived in hope? Even if the worst statistics became reality, an attitude of gloom would only deepen the tragedy, while faith might bring complete or partial healing—at the very least it would make the reality bearable. As I watched the ducks, I vowed to live on the sunny side of the statistical ledger, to always hope and expect the best.

The ducks' wings were feathered and strong for flight when I brought our baby home from the hospital. Even if Lou had not been nine pounds of health and wholeness, we would have loved her just the same. With hope, we would have done all possible to help her fulfill her potential.

To live on the sunny side of the ledger—this is the truth I learned the day the ducks came home.

Wild Kingdom

PAULA WILSHE

$\mathcal{S}$everal weeks ago our sleek and sweet black cat, Kethry, gave birth to three intricately marked tabby kittens. While we were well aware of the probability of her impending motherhood (she had begun to walk with a maternal sway and get stuck in tight spaces) no one was really sure when conception had taken place, so we were not certain when the blessed event might actually happen. Late one Saturday evening I noted that I had not seen her for several hours. A systematic search of the house produced no results until I entered Brett's room. Despite my calls Kethry did not appear, but there emanated a loud purring noise from under Brett's bed.

Although I encourage Brett to remove items from underneath his bed on a regular basis, I am usually placated with an, "As soon as I finish this level," as he soars to new heights in Nintendoland. Brett is very good at video games, and surmises correctly that in the three hours it takes him to "finish the level" (or perhaps several levels, whatever a level is, I don't understand video games) I will have succumbed to new and different housekeeping challenges, and will have forgotten what I asked him to do in the first place.

I suspected that the maternity ward resided somewhere amongst the collection of boxer shorts, unmatched socks, and

G.I. Joe accessories that cover the floor space under the bed, so I was flying blind, reaching my hand in gingerly in hopes that I might connect with warm furry kittens and not impale myself on a plastic sword or combat implement of some kind. After a few tries I was rewarded with the scratchy lick of Kethry's tongue, and the purring became even louder.

Carefully I felt around her for tiny babies, and pulled out the three newborns, gently laying them down on the rug. Kethry followed, winding herself around me, and licking the kittens intermittently, waiting for the praise she clearly felt was indicated. I oohed and ahhed, telling her what a wonderful job she had done, then brought in the flannel-sheet lined basket I had previously prepared for this moment and put first the kittens, then Kethry, inside it.

Kethry seemed pleased with the nursery. She settled back and nursed the squeaking kittens for several minutes, narrowing her eyes in ecstatic maternal bliss. A few moments later my best friend, and the children's adopted aunt, Claudia, returned Brett from an all day excursion to the Washington Zoo. I motioned them to follow, and they tiptoed into the room to view the new arrivals. Kethry was thrilled with the entrance of a freshly appreciative audience. She leaned back, still purring loudly, so they could view her family.

Brett expressed some concern that the kittens were to be in his room, but I assured him that Kethry had paid him a great compliment by selecting this place to give birth. She obviously trusted him and felt comfortable enough to deposit her kittens there. Claudia silenced me with a look when I mentioned something about the unfortunate state of Brett's under-bed area, feeling that this was simply not the time to tarnish the miracle of birth with a lecture on neatness.

Although Kethry seemed to approve of the laundry basket/ bassinet, she did spend the next twenty-four hours moving the kittens around to various areas underneath the bed, as if sampling alternative sites in case the need should arise. She moved them two at a time, rotating the order so that each kitten had several turns under the bed, and the occasional turn remaining in the basket. Unfortunately at this young age the kittens felt both that there was unity in safety, and security in having mom in the feelable vicinity. Therefore, the kitten left in the basket would wail mournfully as Kethry moved its siblings, and when she returned to comfort the kitten alone, the two under the bed would set up a pitiful howl. This did not allow Brett much uninterrupted sleeping time.

He and I fished kittens from under the bed numerous times, and replaced them in the basket. For one twenty-four hour period, Kethry did not move any kittens anywhere, and we were pleased, feeling that the worst was probably over.

On the fourth morning Brett staggered into the kitchen looking haggard. He slouched down in a chair and announced, "Well, Kethry has a new game, Mom."

"What game is that?" I asked, leafing through the morning paper.

"It's called, 'Let's Deposit the Kittens on Brett's Head While He's Sleeping.'"

It seemed that all night long Kethry had gone back and forth between the basket and Brett's bed, and Brett had spent much of the overnight period peeling kittens off his face. I tried to make the situation seem better.

"Brett, you know. . . ."

He held up his hand. "Yes, Mom, I know. Kethry trusts you. That's why she had the kittens in your room. Kethry loves you.

That's why she keeps bringing the kittens on your bed. I'm sorry, Mom, but it doesn't help at three o'clock in the morning." Not a bad assessment from an eleven-year-old.

Thankfully, that was the last night the kittens were mobilized. Perhaps Kethry realized she had pushed Brett to his limit. The next several weeks were quiet. The kittens grew and plumped up on milk from their rigorous nursing schedule. They opened their eyes and began to stagger around the basket. They began to recognize us, and would come to the side of the basket for attention whenever we entered the room.

Our dog Logan kept up a regular vigil at basketside, often sitting and watching the kittens if Kethry strolled out for a snack or a breath of fresh air. Kethry was thankful for the baby-sitting, and would purr and twine herself around his legs in gratitude. The only incident of the next week or so was when my girlfriend Judy and her dog Foster stopped by one afternoon. Foster comes to our house often, and since he and Logan are great friends, naturally Logan took him into the nursery to show off his kittens. Suddenly there was a shriek and a hiss (from Kethry) and a yelp (from Foster.)

Sweet, benevolent Kethry catapulted out of the basket and began chasing Foster around the house, keeping up a howl. Claudia picked up a broom and tried to separate them, but all we could see were whirling masses of black fur flying through the air. Poor Judy had gone to the bathroom and kept yelling, "I'm coming! I'll be right there!" as she struggled to pull her pants up. The ugly incident ended when I grabbed Kethry and tossed her in the room with the kittens, shutting the door quickly. I heard her hurling her body at the door, trying desperately to come back for another round.

Foster cowered behind Judy, blood dripping off his muzzle

from Kethry's scratches. Logan, ever the gracious host, was mortified at this breach of etiquette, and hovered near Foster looking apologetic. Eventually everyone calmed down, although Judy claims that to this day whenever they drive past the house, Foster hides under the seat of the truck. I'm sure she's exaggerating.

All too soon the kittens were growing up, jumping out of the basket and pouncing and rolling around in the clean socks and boxer shorts Brett had thoughtfully left on the floor rather than put them away in their proper drawers. They learned how to eat cat food, and how to sip water. Happily they learned how to use a litter pan, although they were not adverse to tossing occasional but numerous grains of litter onto the rug just for kicks.

Of all the mother cats I've had in my lifetime, Kethry was by far the most attentive. She is the only one I've had who has felt a need to actually *teach* her kittens things. I thought this was a wonderful maternal attribute, and did not hesitate to tell anyone who would listen about this spectacular new mother.

One morning when I staggered to the kitchen for coffee, there was a dead mouse on the floor. I didn't think all that much of it, we live on a farm, after all, and mice come with the territory. I scooped it up in a paper towel and threw it in the trash. Taking my coffee and an article I was writing out to the back porch, I could hear Kethry howling from somewhere inside the house. I walked through to see if she was all right . . . and nearly stepped on *another* dead rodent, but this time the kittens were busy playing volleymouse and quickly tossed it to the other side of the room.

Later that afternoon I happened to look out the door and I saw Kethry galloping down the back yard holding another mouse in her mouth. With a practiced air she trotted down the cellar steps, through the hole that the flood left (a whole other story) and up the kitchen steps where she deposited it for her babies. There was a lot of growling and jumping, as the kittens engaged in an exercise that could only be named the "Dead Shrew Hurl."

Over the next few days Kethry continued to sharpen the kittens' hunting skills by actually bringing the animals in alive and letting them go. I would walk in to find rodents flung about with reckless abandon, lively games of volleyrat, or else find the little hunters sated, nursing drunkenly next to little tidbits of fur, the only remnant of whatever prey had been captured.

From mice and shrews, and there were many, she moved on to rabbits, and finally to the bird group. You have no idea how loud the crunch of fresh bird bones can be at five in the morning. Or how slippery are little piles of feathers when you are in bare feet.

I suppose I should be grateful. As the kittens go to their new homes, I am sure they will earn their keep, and I know the one we are keeping will be a wonderful barn cat and mouser. It's been a terrific experience for everyone, watching these new lives grow and develop and learn. We've had fun with the kittens at every stage, and marveled over their sweetness, intelligence, and affectionate natures. I've been telling Claudia lately how very glad I am that this happened, because I feel that watching nature take its course has been so very enjoyable, informative, and absolutely no trouble at all.

Next week I am having Kethry spayed.

Business Partners

SUSAN McCULLOUGH

For her hostessing job at a world-famous restaurant, all Rose wears is a string of pearls. But when she glides through the lobby to greet diners, people don't notice her lack of clothing. They're more likely to be surprised that she has four legs.

Rose is a dalmatian—and one reason why people love the Inn at Little Washington.

"The response to Rose has been incredible," reports Reinhardt Lynch, co-owner of the five-star establishment in Washington, Virginia. "You wouldn't believe how many people come to the restaurant and ask us if Rose is coming that evening."

Rose is in good company. All over the United States, business people are finding that pets are good for their business.

Although the Inn's cuisine draws rave reviews from critics and diners alike, Rose may be almost as big a draw as the food. Co-owner and head chef Patrick O'Connell thinks he knows why.

"Having Rose work out front is a real ice-breaker," O'Connell explains. "Many people have preconceptions about fancy restaurants; they think they're stuffy and pretentious. A dog melts those preconceptions away."

Kurt and Lisa Lidtke, of Seattle, Washington, would probably agree. They've found that their two weimaraners, Griffin and Willow, help relax visitors to their art gallery.

"Art galleries can be rather intimidating," explains Lisa. "But people who see our dogs in the gallery start talking immediately. We end up talking to people who might otherwise not know how to start a conversation with us. Having the dogs here creates a much friendlier atmosphere and puts people at ease."

Both the Inn at Little Washington and the Kurt Lidtke Gallery have capitalized on their dogs' popularity. The Inn's gift shop abounds with products inspired by Rose and her dalmatian buddy DeSoto: dalmatian bookends, dal-spotted neckties, a cookie mix named after Rose, postcards of Rose clad in a pearl-and-ruby necklace.

The Lidtkes announce upcoming shows by mailing their clients postcards of Griffin and Willow sitting in front of the gallery. "The postcards really help position us with respect to our competition," says Lisa. "People know that we're the gallery with the dogs."

The Lidtkes never planned to market their gallery through Griffin and Willow. "We started bringing our dogs because we didn't want to leave them home alone all day," Lisa says.

A similar concern prompted the owners of the Vienna Sewing Machine and Vacuum Center to start bringing their black Labrador retriever puppy, Abby, to their Vienna, Virginia, shop 11 years ago. But Abby's presence turned out to be great for business. "Some people come to the store just to see her," co-owner Jim Sabo gladly admits.

Some of Abby's fans bring her dog cookies and other gifts when they come to visit. And more often than not, visitors leave with at least a few more vacuum cleaner bags than they'd planned to purchase.

Other dogs go corporate when their entrepreneurial owners do. That's what happened with Rags, an Old English sheepdog who commutes with owners Cynthia Black and Richard Cohn to Beyond Words Publishing, the Hillsboro, Oregon, company Black and Cohn founded.

The couple started Beyond Words in their home, where Rags' presence posed no problem. When Black and Cohn moved to commercial office space, they got their landlord's approval to bring Rags with them. Today, the company Web site includes a page and e-mail box for Rags, who's described as the "official office greeter, company mascot, and furry friend." Says Black, "Rags makes people who visit our company more comfortable—and makes the company a warmer place to work."

Other companies deliberately include animals in their corporate families. Several years ago, the Iams Company of Dayton, Ohio, selected Kersee, a female golden retriever, to be the pet food manufacturer's vice president of canine communications. Today, 6-year-old Kersee greets visitors and represents Iams at public events.

Kersee undertook rigorous training before assuming her duties. Once Kersee's formal instruction was completed, her trainer sent Iams employees a list of "Kersee Rules and Regulations" that details the 30-odd commands the dog knows. Those commands range from the basic come-sit-stay to more complex skills such as not shaking off water while being bathed.

The Lidtke Gallery's Griffin and Willow also received formal training, after which Kurt and Lisa Lidtke taught the dogs proper gallery deportment, such as not barking on the job and refraining from jumping on visitors. "Occasionally, they'll wander over and sniff people who come into the gallery, but that's about it," says Lisa.

The Inn at Little Washington's Rose boarded for two weeks with a local trainer before becoming a hostess. She, too, has learned to refrain from barking while at work. In addition, she doesn't enter the dining room unless O'Connell or Lynch invites her to do so.

Training alone doesn't make a dog ready to work, though. The Inn's other dalmatian, DeSoto, trained with Rose but never equaled her on-the-job success.

"Once when he was a puppy, DeSoto ran into the dining room and jumped up onto the banquette where a woman was already seated," O'Connell recalls. "Then he ate the lobster she ordered." The woman didn't mind—in fact, she kept the pup seated next to her until the kitchen could prepare a new lobster for her. Nowadays, though, O'Connell and Lynch generally leave DeSoto home.

from PETS: PART OF THE FAMILY

Babe in the Woods

SHARI SMYTH

"**Y**ou know what's missing?" I said to my husband, Whitney. It was a warm evening, and the two of us were lounging on our long, low front porch, looking out over the yard. Our cats, Sheba and Bucci, played at our feet.

"I can't imagine," Whitney said, loafers propped on a stool.

"The kids," I said. "I wish they could pop in for dinner."

"Well, they can't. They live too far away."

"What I meant was—"

"I know what you meant," he interrupted, moving closer. "We've had this conversation before. You want our kids to move here to Tennessee. Having them so far away worries you."

"It does," I said. I had never gotten used to being a long-distance mom.

Our son, Jon, lived in Maine. Recently he'd gone camping in the northern part of the state and was supposed to have returned two days earlier. We hadn't heard from him. Every time I called I got the message on his answering machine: "Can't come to the phone right now." Something might have happened to him.

When I'd last spoken to our daughter Wendy, she was upset because she'd just broken up with her boyfriend. "I really need a hug from you, Mom," she'd told me on the phone. I wished I could hop into the car and get to her, but Hawaii was a long drive from Tennessee.

And Sanna was in Florida and Laura was all the way in Oregon. Sure, they had jobs and friends. They phoned and even visited once in a while. Still I worried, and it was hard to know if my prayers for them had any effect.

"They're good kids," Whitney reminded me. "They can take care of themselves. You need to accept that."

"Easy for you to say. You're not their mother," I retorted as the phone rang.

I dashed into the house to answer it, tripping over the cats' food dish on the way. It was Jon. "Hey, Mom. Camping was great. I got back a few days ago. Sorry I forgot to call."

"I was worried," I said, an edge to my voice.

"Mom, I can take care of myself. Honest," he replied.

Can he really? Sighing, I returned to the porch. I reached for the cat food dish at the top of the steps, but froze when I noticed something lurking in the bushes. A scrawny calico cat looked out from the branches, staring at the food, whiskers twitching.

"It's all right," I said softly, setting down the dish and backing into the house. I watched through the window. The cat crept up the steps and peered around, a hunted, haunted look on her face. Her dull coat stretched taut over her jutting bones. She devoured the food, then took off. The next night she returned, and the next, and the one after that.

"We have a new cat," I told Whitney. "I've named her Babe."

He laughed. "I hope *she* lets you know where she is after dark."

The fifth night it was raining. When the cat poked her head above the steps, I was waiting. In the dry shelter of the porch,

I'd placed a bed of towels and a dish of tuna. "Come here, Babe," I coaxed. "I won't hurt you." She crept toward the food, fur standing almost straight up. Stretching her neck, she began to nibble. Gingerly I scratched the wet fur between her ears. She stiffened, then relaxed. *Whitney was right,* I thought. *Now I have someone else to worry about.*

During the next few weeks reports came in from the kids: Laura was fighting a cold; Sanna was having roommate problems; Wendy had a date with a new guy. And I had Babe. She came daily, eating from the dish of food I put out. Her calico coat thickened and began to shine. She stretched out on the wooden porch, falling asleep on her back. I planned to take her to the vet to get fixed, but one autumn day she didn't show up for her usual meal. I drove around looking for her. I hiked, checking the woods. I left food out all night. When it remained untouched, I imagined the worst.

But as Christmas approached I had to put Babe out of my mind. My children were coming home! For the first time in two years I had all four of them under one roof. They filled the house with good news: Laura had a steady beau; Sanna and Jon had both gotten promotions; Wendy had a new cottage overlooking the ocean. And for a whole glorious week I wasn't a long-distance mom.

One night at dinner I ventured, "Why don't you all consider relocating to Tennessee? Dad and I can help with the move and finding jobs. You could live here till you found a place." Forks clattered to the table, and everyone fell silent.

Finally Sanna spoke: "Maybe someday, Mom. But for now we're happy where we are."

By week's end the kids had all gone. The house felt empty. And whenever I stepped onto the porch, there was no calico cat sneaking in from the woods to feast at the food dish. All I had for my children, and that undomesticated cat, were my prayers—and worries.

Then, on a raw, wet late-March evening I found Babe huddled on the porch mat. I was thrilled to see her, until I took a closer look. Her coat was dull and scraggly. She was pregnant, and obviously due any day. "You poor thing," I said, stroking her gently. She mewed meekly.

I fed her, toweled her off and lined a waterproof crate with throw rugs. "There's your nursery," I informed her. Babe sniffed the crate and curled up inside it. I stood watching her, feeling nervous like an expectant grandmother.

On April Fool's Day I opened the door to find a newly sleek Babe. "Congratulations, Mama. Where's your brood?" But the joke was on me. I looked in the crate. Empty. I shone a flashlight under the porch. No kittens. I looked everywhere. "Where are they?" I fretted as I brought Babe her breakfast. She ate, washed herself, then stretched out to nap. I went inside. When I came out a minute later, Babe was gone.

I called the vet. "I have to find those kittens before something happens to them!"

"You might as well give up," he said. "It's out of your control. Trust her instincts."

Fat chance, I thought. I tramped through the woods. I looked under logs, in a woodpile, in an old abandoned shed. I rooted through piles of dead leaves. Turkey vultures circled high above me. I shuddered to think what might have happened.

Yet in the following weeks every morning Babe continued to come by for breakfast, then slip away. While she ate I worried about those kittens. What was I going to do? Hadn't I tried everything? Babe washed her whiskers and her ears, looking at me sideways. "Trust her instincts," the vet had said.

Suddenly it seemed so simple. Trust. That was the one thing I hadn't tried. Trust Babe. Trust my children. Trust God.

One day Jon called. "Guess what, Mom? The guys and me are planning a trip to India. We're going to quit our jobs and go for two months."

I gripped the counter, picturing my son lost in Calcutta, all his money spent. *Trust, Shari. Trust.* When I opened my mouth, I heard myself say, "This is the time of life to do those things . . . before you settle down and have a family."

There was a stunned silence at the other end of the line. Then, "Thanks, Mom. I was kind of dreading telling you." I think I surprised Jon as much as I surprised myself.

Speaking of surprised, on a balmy May afternoon I opened the door and there was Babe with three adorable, orange tabby kittens. Mama looked up at me with a cat grin that said, "Here they are, all healthy." Three boys I named Billy, Bobby and Tommy. They live with their mom on my porch.

"Just wait till *we* show up with kids someday," Sanna joked. I'm waiting, peacefully for once, trusting God.

The Godsend

MARK LUCE

$\mathcal{M}$eet Twinky: Irish Wolfhound, service dog, godsend. On all fours she stands as tall as a kitchen table—33 inches—and weighs 110 pounds. At 9 years old she responds to commands in German and Spanish, and also understands some Russian, English and hand signals.

Her job and passion: Give physical and mental support to her owner, Renate Whalen of Santa Clarita, Calif. "We have a special bond," said Whalen, who suffers from chronic pain as a result of a double hip-replacement surgery gone wrong about 20 years ago. "She's very calm, quiet and not a nervous dog at all. And she calms me, too."

Whalen, who had trained horses and worked as a stunt woman before her hip surgery, was living in the Austrian Alps in 1991 when she purchased 3-month-old Twinky from a Czechoslovakian breeder. "I lived alone in a big house in the forest and needed a lot of help getting around," she said.

Whalen immediately started Twinky in obedience school (the dog would complete three obedience courses) and augmented that training with the help of a neighbor, a man who purchased and trained dogs for the Vienna police.

After about 20 months, Twinky was ready to be a service dog. She was able to help Whalen steady herself and navigate the craggy landscape, slippery roads and snow piles in the icy mountain region. If Whalen slipped and fell, Twinky, clad in a flashing collar and reflective vest, blocked oncoming traffic and provided a shoulder to help Whalen lift herself to her feet.

In town they'd rest at the local café, where Whalen taught Twinky the behavior she uses today in public places, especially restaurants: head down, tail down and under the table. Despite her size, she can be inconspicuous. "She becomes invisible," Whalen said. "She won't focus her stare or make funny noises in public."

However, she does know how to make friends in public. In the early 1990s, a handful of Bosnian refugees relocated to Whalen's village. Still shocked and scared by the carnage they had seen, the children took a shine to Twinky. "Twinky's size helped the children from Bosnia feel protected as they walked her," Whalen said. "They learned they didn't have to be afraid in this new country. She helped their self-confidence."

Twinky helps Whalen's self-confidence, too. People often look strangely at her and Twinky, mainly because of the dog's size. But once Whalen explains Twinky's role as a service dog, people tend to warm up. "People are pretty understanding when they know Twinky is there to help me," Whalen said. "They see how she helps me along."

Twinky came to the United States in 1998, when Whalen and her husband Richard were married. The dog traveled without a hitch—navigating international airports, changing planes, flying in first class and even allowing another passenger to warm her feet beneath her thick fur.

Complications arose after they landed in California. Twice, they were forced to leave restaurants despite the Americans with Disabilities Act, which guarantees disabled people the right to take service animals into public accommodations.

"It was so embarrassing to be thrown out," Whalen said, adding that she successfully sued one restaurant, which subsequently posted signs and instructed employees to welcome disabled people and their service dogs.

"We weren't out for money," Richard Whalen said. "We only wanted to make sure it doesn't happen to anybody else."

Twinky has accompanied Whalen to many restaurants and hotels without incident. "She's the perfect size for me to lean on her instead of using a cane," she said. "People are really astonished by her. She doesn't get scared, she isn't dangerous and she watches out for me."

When off duty, Twinky sniffs around the yard, or curls up on her bed of pillows, blankets and a fluffy, old jacket in the living room. "Twinky is part of the family," Richard Whalen said. "She's got a great personality and performs a wonderful service for Renate."

Without Twinky, Whalen would probably have to rely on her wheelchair. "I can't imagine being without her," she said. "I don't know how I would get along. I would be very insecure, would feel unsafe and helpless. She's my buddy. She's my shadow, and she's terrific."

from DOG FANCY

Clare's Story

JAN ROGERS

Clare came into the world on Mother's Day, along with eight other little chicks, hatched out in a neighbor's incubator. All of them were precious and perfect, except for Clare, who was far from perfect, but more precious than words can say. It was her legs—oh, her poor little twisted legs, which went this way and that; in every direction but any that would do her any good.

When I first saw her I took myself on an all-expenses-paid Guilt Trip. Was she deformed because of the incubator? It was unnatural. What if I caused her to suffer by letting the chicken's eggs go into the incubator along with my neighbor's turkey eggs? Maybe the incubator worked better if it was filled, but at whose expense? Clare's?

It made no sense. All of the others were fine; only Clare was cursed with crippled legs. What kind of life could she have, with legs that would never walk?

The men said, "You should put it out of its misery." The women said, "No. Wait and see if she can get around. Give her a chance."

Being a woman, I wanted to wait and see. Just the thought of taking a chick whose body was about the size of a cotton ball and . . . what? Crushing her? Wringing her tiny neck? Suffocating her in a plastic bag? How did the men intend to end the misery that I wasn't so sure she was in? No! There would be plenty of time for untender mercies later, and if it came to that, I would have the vet do it.

The men laughed and laughed. "You'd take a chicken to a vet? You're kidding, right?"

I boxed up my new babies and took them home, the men shaking their heads as I drove away.

Clare couldn't walk, but that didn't stop her from getting around, even though she seemed to navigate by nothing more than her own will. My main concern was that the other chicks would begin to pick on her, to peck at her, which is normal chicken behavior. If that happened, I'd have to decide if raising a flock animal in isolation was crueler than death. But it never came to that. The other chicks not only left her alone, they actually got out of her way when she was trying to get to food or water. And her way was the long way around; she used her wings as legs and her legs sometimes as rudders, sometimes as obstacles to overcome, depending on the position they happened to be in.

The camaraderie the other chicks shared with Clare only intensified as they grew older. Lilly, so named because she was white when she hatched, seemed to be Clare's special friend and protector. Clare was a beautiful mixture of white blending to pale blond blending to a lovely honey color. As Lilly grew, it became apparent that a new name was in order, because Lilly was obviously turning into a beautiful rooster with coloring similar to Clare's. So Lilly became Louie, and the young chickens got big enough to go outside with the other older chickens, and feel the sweet green grass beneath them.

At first Clare, sensing her own vulnerability, wouldn't venture outside with the other chickens; she preferred to stay inside the chicken house, playing it safe beneath the lawn mower. She managed to hop, flop, and fly her way around the floor to get to where she wanted to go. I felt sorry for her always being left behind, so I started spending time with her. She was sweet and friendly, and she loved to be in my lap to eat treats out of my hand and be stroked and talked to. Her favorite spot was the top of her head. A gentle finger or thumb stroking her head always made her beg for more, and start her chirping in reply to my words and songs. Head stroking led to her settling down in my lap for a nap in the sun.

Sometimes I took her outside, so that she could enjoy the feel, taste and smell of the grass, and the unlucky bug who wasn't paying attention and landed too near her. Before long she was venturing out every day, gallantly trying to be just another chicken. She went where they went, and gave me fits when she would go where no other chicken would dare to go.

I heard her cry for help once when I went to shut them up for the night, but I couldn't find her. I kept calling her, and she kept answering me until I followed her chirps to the tiny space beneath the hen house with its block foundation. I ran to get the flashlight—there might be snakes under there—and, belly-to-the-ground, peered in and saw her. She was stuck, stopped by rocks and dirt and the floor of the hen house above her. She'd peep and leap, peep and leap, but it got her nowhere. She was too far back for me to reach her, and I started to cry.

I dashed into the house, frantically thinking of how to get her out. I got a broom, an umbrella and a coat hanger, and ran back outside. I had to use all three to maneuver her to where I could finally reach in and grab her. She was dirty, wet and tired, so I brought her inside to clean and warm her up before returning her to the chicken house for the night. Then I closed up the holes that led to the dark and dangerous space under there.

Time passed, and Clare continued to delight and amaze me. I thought she would grow up with the other chickens and even begin to lay eggs, but I was wrong. Clare was nearly four months old when I found her dead in the hen house one morning, the victim of a huge blacksnake who had somehow squeezed in. The snake had swallowed her, head first, up to her shoulders, but she was too big for it to eat, so it had spit her out.

I cried and cried and blamed myself for not knowing that this could happen. I didn't know that snakes will kill what they can't eat, and I no longer tolerate them in or around the chicken house.

I still miss that sweet little crippled chicken with her brave heart and her strong will to live. Clare taught me much in her short, valiant life. She taught me not to give up when it seems that there is no hope; she taught me that no life is insignificant or without value, and that even a little chicken like Clare could take up a huge space in my heart, just by letting her in.

One

GENE HILL

I admired the dog out of courtesy and that was about it. He wasn't anything special to look at—just your nice, solid, big-headed black Lab. I've seen hundreds just like him, give or take an inch here or a detail there. His work in the field was efficient, but not exciting. He wasn't what a real trial man would call steady and as often as not he'd drop a goose to readjust a hold; generally preferring to drag it along by a wing. He did have one peculiar habit I noticed—he never picked up a bird, no matter how dead it was without stepping on the neck with one foot first and holding it there until he'd grabbed the wing. I asked about this, and his owner told me that it was a habit he'd had from the first, since his first goose had picked him pretty bad. This bit of cause and effect reasoning pleased me being a "once burned, twice shy" person myself.

This day in a goose pit on the eastern shore of Maryland was as common as the surrounding mud. Intermittent flights had us calling, more for the amusement of it than any real hope of turning them. But every so often a pair or a small flock of five or six would toll close enough for a shot and since we were in no hurry or that anxious to take geese, we took turns gunning. By mid-afternoon we each had two geese—enough for our personal satisfaction, but the weather was mild so we had come to a mutual unspoken agreement to just sit there and chat rather than pick up and go our separate ways. It was a lovely way to spend an afternoon—gunning talk mostly, a little fishing talk, some book titles exchanged—just your average small talk between two relative strangers who found common ground and an occasional bit of laughter that sweetened the conversation, putting each of us at ease and wanting the other to find us good company . . . a small, pleasant spontaneous friendship.

He hardly mentioned his Lab, and neither did I, but I was pleased to notice the dog sat leaning a little against his master's leg or put his head on his foot when he chose to lie down, and that my companion's hand was stroking the dog or messing with his ears or scratching him behind the neck. It was just the sort of thing any one of us might do, an ordinary circumstance, a common-place relationship. Nor did I find it strange the dog paid absolutely no attention to me whatsoever. There are dogs that are nuisances for affection (several of mine are like that from being spoiled and encouraged to play) and others that like to keep to themselves, and others that are clearly one-person creatures.

He had not bothered to bring a lunch, and I, for once, had gotten myself together and packed one. As usual, when I do get a lunch-making urge, I tend to go overboard and had more than enough to share, which I gladly did. We each had two sandwiches, and as he ate he fed the other to the dog at the same pace, bite for bite. A sandwich and a half was enough for me, so I offered the dog the half left over. He wouldn't touch it from my hand, so I placed it on the floor of the blind in front of him where it sat unnoticed and untasted until I asked my friend if the dog was on some sort of self-imposed diet.

"No, I don't think so," he laughed, and picked up the food and as before fed it to the dog bite by bite.

You can usually sense when someone has been waiting for a chance to talk about something that needs to be aired. You feel he's been looking for the right time and place and ear. I was hoping that I'd have that privilege, so I just sat there and watched him dribble pieces of that sandwich, pieces about the size of 00 Buck, to a dog that was not only used to this little game, but so delighted with it that he was making soft moaning noises and rolling his eyes. . . .

"Pete, here, is about the worst dog I've ever owned," he said with some hesitation, "but he's taught me more about dogs, in a strange way, than most of the others I've had—and there have been quite a few."

I just sat there and stared at the floor of the blind, not wanting to look at him, because he didn't want to look at me . . . right now he wanted a listener, a sympathetic and understanding one—one who had some of the knowledge of what he was talking about, but not a conversation—just the ear would do fine for the time being.

"If you've ever followed the big field trial circuit you'd probably know my name. For quite a few years I was the amateur trainer that most of the pros worried about. And they had good reason. I had the money, the time, the drive and the dogs. And you needed all that just to start because you were in against the Belmonts, the Roosevelts, big steel money, big oil money and just plain money so big that hardly anyone remembered where it all had come from. One handler drove his dogs to the trials in an old Rolls Royce fitted up like a kennel truck; the people he worked for drove Rolls' and they didn't want their dogs in anything less! I didn't go that far . . . but I wasn't too far behind. I've chartered more than one plane to take my dogs where I thought they ought to be running, and I've never regretted a penny of it.

"I even had Purdey make me a pair of side-bys just for field trial gunning in case my dogs didn't finish so I'd still be part of the action—and you learn a lot about certain dogs when you're a gun—but that's getting a little away from my story.

"It all started simply enough—and typically as far as I'm concerned. I've always loved competition—I've been a top flight amateur golfer, a tournament winner on the trap and skeet circuit, and got to where they knew I was there in the live bird rings of Madrid and Monte Carlo. Then I got to thinking about getting a dog. I traveled so much in my early days that owning one didn't make much sense. My hosts, when I went shooting, all had fine kennels so it didn't make any difference if I had any or not. In fact it was better that I didn't. But when a big holding company bought me out for more money than I could ever spend and moved me up to some spot that was all title and no work, I began to look around for something new to take up. It was just about destiny that I'd start field trialing Labs.

"I'd been a member of one of those fancy Long Island duck clubs for years and had seen some pretty good dogs. It might sound silly, but I believe that a man has to have a dog and a breed of dog that suits his personality. If I believed in reincarnation I don't doubt that I'd come back as a Lab—or would like to. It's a little vain I know, but I saw myself as brave, honest and strong, as Hemingway might have put it, and that's what I like about the Lab. It's all up front, nothing held back.

"Anyway, one of my duck hunting buddies at the old Sprig Club had a litter of dogs out of good field trial stock and he gave me a male as sort of a retirement present. He said that at worst he'd be somebody I could talk to and take care of and get the same in return. After I'd spent a few weeks with the pup I decided to have a professional take a look at him. I felt that he might have what it would take to be a trial dog, but I believe in the opinions of the people who do it every day, not just an amateur appraisal.

"The professional not only liked the dog but made an offer then and there to take him for training, and I agreed. He had a fine reputation and I liked his whole approach to the training idea. He was to start the dog, and when he was satisfied I'd come down and spend a week or so with him and learn to run the dog myself. Then I'd get a training schedule to work on and check back with him for a few days on a regular basis. If the dog did exceptionally well, he'd take him over completely and campaign in the major stakes. His name was Wonderdog—because I wondered what I'd do with him when I first got him; a little joke with myself. If you follow the retrievers you know how far he got and what a piece of pure bad luck it was he didn't become National Champion. He was killed a little while after his first Nationals—an assistant trainer was in an accident and the dog trailer was totally demolished. I was hurt by the loss, of course, but by then I'd been committed to try for another dog as good as he was. He'd sired a litter and I arranged to get the pick for stud service.

"If anything, he was better than his father; a bit more aggressive and strangely a bit more biddable. It was almost as if he felt destined to compete and understood what was expected of him all along. I called him Little Wonder—another private joke with myself. Almost everyone was soon calling him One, short for number one because that's what he looked like right from the start. He was one of the hottest derby dogs anyone had seen when he was right, and he usually was. I'd never thought of a dog as an athlete before One, but when he took to water he reminded me of a diver—I know it's silly to think of a dog having 'form' but he did—and I never got over the idea that he knew it and worked at it.

"By the time he was three, One had totally captivated the trial circuit—not just in wins and placements, but by his personality—his pure competitiveness and genius for doing just the right thing at the right time. I know for sure that more than one judge laid out a series with just him in mind, but as hard as they tried to challenge him he was usually up to it. Of course he had an off-day now and then, disinterested or bored or maybe tired, but even then he did his job, but without the fire he was famous for. In his first National at Bombay Hook he placed third. I don't think he deserved to win, but I think he deserved at least second. The head judge and I weren't exactly friends, since I'd beaten his dog at several important trials and he wasn't above playing a little politics with some nationally known names.

"I'd planned to retire One after his first in the Nationals, and just use him as a stud dog and gunning companion. We'd become pretty close and I thought he deserved a little rest and some fun—and some fun had long gone out of the competition as far as I was concerned. But I did want that win for him in the worst way. He'd worked hard for it and most of us still believed that he had the class and the talent to go all the way; if any dog deserved it, One certainly did. The more we worked him that season the sharper he got. I didn't think that there was much room for improvement, but in subtle ways he just looked better. His long blinds were precision itself and when he was stopped to the whistle he really stopped. It was as if he was reading your mind—I heard one judge remark in a friendly way that he looked as if he were showing off. I'm making him sound as if he were absolutely perfect, but he did have one small fault. Not in every trial, but every now and then for some reason he'd make one or two little yelps on a retrieve on land. I always put it down as pure enthusiasm and the trainer and I had long given up on trying to make him stop. More often than not, we'd be the only ones to notice it."

Here he paused for so long I didn't think he was going to go on with the rest of the story. He was rumpling his dog and searching for the right words and the strength to say them. I had the feeling that this was a story that he'd never told before and perhaps didn't want to—yet knew that he must so he could get a different grip on it himself. For some strange reason I thought of the words to an old song about "hanging your tears out to dry"—how perfectly put, how perfectly true.

For the first time since he'd begun, he turned to look at me and I could see the gray, sad sparkle of small tears. I turned away a bit to give him a moment of privacy. He covered his face with his handkerchief for just a second and went on.

"I'd say the chances of what happened ever happening are more than one in a million. One of those random tragedies that seem to strike the innocent; the casual passerby. There was a strand of wire, just one, that was only about two feet long between an old post and a tree. I'd heard One making his odd yipping noise and suddenly he went end over end in the air and lay still. Both the judges and I rushed out knowing instantly that something fearful had happened, and there was One stretched out, dead from a broken neck. A small trickle of blood ran down the corners of his jaw where he'd run into the wire with his mouth open.

"I carried him back to the station wagon and put him on

the front seat and started to drive. I don't remember how long it was or where I went, but I do remember that I kept rubbing his head believing for the longest time that he'd suddenly sit up and everything would be all right. Today is only the second time in my life that I've cried; that was the first.

"There's a small graveyard behind the lodge at the Sprig Club where our special dogs were put to rest and the whole club turned out to help me put him there. I had a blanket made of his ribbons and my gunning coat was his pillow. He always loved to sleep on that whenever he had the chance. One of the members read a list of his wins and when finished with that, he paused, and in a soft tenor began to sing Auld Lang Syne and everyone, except me, joined in with him."

He stopped again for a minute and blew his nose; I must confess I did the same.

"I virtually stopped gunning for a long time after that. When people asked me why, I told them that my favorite partner had passed away and almost none of them ever thought that it might have been just my dog. Funny, isn't it, how few can understand the relationship a man can have with his dog? And yet, I can tell you now that there were few, if any, things in my life that meant as much to me as One, and how odd but true that an emptiness like that is there forever.

"It's been about five years since I lost One and last fall a friend of mine, the same one that sang that afternoon at the duck club, came to my house and rang the bell. When I opened the door he reached in and put a puppy in my arms and said, 'It's about time Pete had someone to look after,' and turned and left.

"This is Pete." At the sound of his name, Pete looked up and made some sort of a face that I'll say was as close to smiling as a dog can get.

"When I said that Pete was the worst of my dogs I didn't mean anything but that I'd never trained him. I just let him be Pete. And that's enough, more than enough. They say that a man deserves one good dog in his life . . . but that's not true. I've had a couple, and in his own way, Pete's right there in my heart with them all now. It's a full space with two empty ones beside it if you can see it that way."

I nodded to let him know that I agreed, but I didn't say anything because I didn't think anything needed to be said just at that moment.

He began, after a little while, to talk about something else and after giving me his card he thanked me for listening and said it was time for him and Pete to be heading on home. I said goodbye and told him that I'd wait here a little while longer in the blind just to watch the sun come down. But that wasn't the whole truth. What I wanted to do was sit there in the quiet of twilight and hear soft phrases of that ancient Scottish melody again in my mind and picture the scene of that group of men singing a dog to eternity and comforting themselves in the timeless ritual of shared sorrow and the understanding of loss.

In the last light, I slung my two geese over my shoulder and started back to where I'd left the car. I found myself softly singing what I could remember of One's funeral song, and surprisingly, I wasn't as saddened by the idea as you'd imagine. The saving thought was one of remembrance; as long as a man lives, so will his dog in one form or another . . . in a story or a song. One will always be there to take care of the other and I can't think of a nicer way to put it than we will "share a cup of kindness now . . . "

from TEARS & LAUGHTER

ALWAYS UNDERSTANDING

"Love is a language which the blind can see and the deaf can hear."

DONALD E. WILDMAN

It's amazing how well animals communicate with us even though they don't speak a word of our language. I don't know anyone who can comfort me as quickly as my dogs and cats when I'm feeling sad. And when I'm ready to celebrate, they're two steps ahead of me. If I need to concentrate on my work, they lie quietly under my desk, or on it, and the steady sound of their breathing makes me feel secure.

I never have to explain myself to them. They just know.

Honey-Bun

ANNE STOCKTON

I live alone with two cats and I love them both, maybe more than would be usual, even though I have many friends and affections around me, and memories of loves that life brought and took away, to whom I remain devoted and grateful. Still, there is something different, so particular and poignant about living with a little creature through whom the whole animal world speaks without speaking . . . without a word.

Souls are stretched to understand each other. Words sometimes cannot pass but understanding can, and in the soul world animals and people can meet, for humans are not so far human as they would like to think! Such a little one is a whole education as well as companion, friend and comforter.

But Honey-Bun I loved especially, for I never knew, and I have known many, such a Perfect Cat, almost on the way to becoming human. We understood each other. He taught me love, compassion; body language whether human or animal, and also, what I should have given to my children and was too scared, too immature at twenty to fulfill or even conceive. The complexity of life!

from HONEY-BUN

Lowell

GAY L. BALLIET

One of the conditions I set for agreeing to marry my husband, Edgar, was, "Thou shalt provide me with hordes of pets." And "hordes" it became, as almost directly after coming back from our honeymoon, I began my animal collection. During the years since we were married, I have accumulated a menagerie of animals rivaling Dr. Doolittle's. Our backyard now resembles Hicks's *The Peaceable Kingdom,* with languid creature eyes peeking out from behind every oak tree and from underneath the rhododendron and mountain laurel lining the driveway.

In the beginning, while Edgar and I were living in a mobile home, I took in my first sickly stray kitten, eyes pussed over and nose leaking. His name was Tuxedo Timmy. He was a special guy who first stole my heart with his charming and eccentric personality. He reminded me of television's old Felix the cat. My relationship with Timmy was just the beginning of my love affair with animals. By the time Edgar finished veterinary school, we had accumulated three horses and another cat. After we moved and built our cottage in the woods, within a few short years I managed to gather upwards of thirty barn cats, ten house cats, two dogs, sundry saltwater fish, a Scotch Highland steer, a donkey, a burro, a llama, an alpaca, seven horses, and, finally, the pièce de résistance—a pig.

Lowell is my pet. He is also the love of my life, much to my husband's chagrin.

The first time I met Lowell I was immediately enthralled. I remember the encounter fondly. That day Edgar had some veterinary work in the Poconos—a honeymoon vacation resort area in eastern Pennsylvania. Whenever he was called upon to doctor animals in the Poconos, I begged to go along, mostly because sometime during the day he would take me to lunch at Henri's restaurant. So, that day, while I patiently accompanied him on his morning calls, I was secretly counting the minutes until I would be tasting Henri's chicken Caesar salad. I love to eat, and that's only one of the things I have in common with pigs. My task was to wait out the veterinary work until lunch time.

"I just have this one call to do before we head up to the Poconos," Edgar said at seven that morning as he pulled the truck into the Conley's driveway.

A red, rectangular, aluminum-sided horse barn loomed out of the morning mist, and beyond it I could barely see three horses standing knee-deep in the marshy grass. The earth was damp with ground fog. We pulled up to the barn and shut off the engine, and when I opened my door, the mist curled lazily inside our truck cab. It was like T.S. Eliot's yellow fog that, cat-like, rubbed its back along the windowpanes. I inhaled the fresh, moist air and noted the particular brand of silence that enfolded this part of the valley. Every sound was muffled. Only the horses shifting in the grass could be heard as they awaited their breakfast.

How still the atmosphere, how unearthly. Yet how sweet and clean the grasses, how pungent the smell of horse manure. The wet air sharpened the senses—made them keener, more discriminating.

"What are you doing at this barn?" I asked, inhaling a deep, moist breath. I stretched and yawned, images of Henri's salad already dancing in my head.

"Just vaccinating a bunch of pigs," Edgar said, rummaging through his truck for vials of vaccines. "It won't take long—about nine pigs in all—then we'll head for the Poconos and Henri's."

"Oh, boy," I said. "Hurry up. I'm starving."

While he gathered the equipment, I sank comfortably into the passenger seat and propped my feet on the dashboard as the waves of mist rolled in through my window. Through the windshield I noticed a low, dark, bulky figure wading through the fog-wrapped weeds by the barn. Whatever it was crawled nearly on the same plane as the worms: it was very short, not much higher than the plants, and it had a low center of gravity—like Steven Spielberg's film creation E.T. And for that moment it looked just as alien. I squinted to make sense of it.

"What's that?" I whispered, the fog swallowing up my words.

"Huh?" Edgar said, staring at the hulk slowly approaching the truck. "Oh," he laughed, "that's Hazel. I forgot to tell you—they're Vietnamese potbellies I'm vaccinating—a litter of babies."

I took my feet off the dashboard and opened the door. "Potbellies? I'm coming along to help," I said with sudden interest. "Henri's can wait."

The mother pig bored through the knee-deep grass and past the barn and headed directly toward us. Her abdomen swayed from one side to the other—first to the east and then to the west—a meaty metronome. Her belly was a pendulous, flaccid sack—not because she was fat, but because she was stretched out of shape from carrying babies and feeding them.

Her teats were full of milk. They dangled only an inch above the ground. In fact, the teats scraped the ground every so often as she maneuvered over grass clumps and hillocks. I winced as she crossed over the newly graveled driveway, its stones rasping her soft underbelly. Hazel strolled alongside the truck and stopped to inspect us. She sat down on her haunches, exposing her red-raw teats, and looked quizzically up at us, emitting a quick, low, contented grunt.

Oddly, I felt compelled to answer her greeting. "Good morning, Hazel. Your poor belly looks sore," I said. "You must have had an awfully heavy load of babies. But don't worry, you'll get your shape back in a few weeks." Then I said to Edgar, "Do pigs bite?" I was completely ignorant of pig behavior.

"Adults can," he said. "It's their natural defense. They grow pretty good-sized teeth, and when they get really annoyed they use them. They can also slash with their tusks if they need to defend themselves against another animal."

"Yikes," I said, regarding the cute, smiling face on this quirky concierge of the barnyard. "She looks friendly enough. Do you think she'll let us into the barn?"

"Yeah, she's a pretty good pig. But I don't know how she's going to handle having her babies vaccinated."

"What's the big deal about getting a shot?" I asked. "How does the mother even know the piglets are getting injections?"

"Oh, you haven't been around pigs much, have you?" Edgar laughed. "Pigs are the over-protective mothers of the animal world. She knows that her babies are just as afraid as she is of any kind of restraint—no matter how innocuous it really is. Pigs always think that no matter what a person does to them, they're dying. And they squeal and scream and carry on until you'd swear they were going to kill themselves with their own hysteria. And you can't try talking them out of their unreasonable fear because to them a situation of restraint is lifethreatening. When you're dealing with pigs and especially pig mommies, the only thing you can do is learn to mentally block out the screaming. And then you just do what you need to do, as fast as you can, and release them." . . .

"Isn't it funny how different animals react differently to veterinary care?" I mused while helping Edgar gather his supplies. "Horses, for example, will take a shot without blinking an eye—most of them, anyway. Cows, too. And dogs and cats, for the most part. But pigs must be natured differently. That's interesting. Are you sure they are reacting solely out of fear, or could they possibly be protesting out of a sense of our taking away their right to control what's happening to them? Or maybe they are expressing pure anger at the restraint. Actually, it could be a number of things the pigs are protesting. Fear might be the obvious one, but I thought pigs were supposed to be intelligent. Maybe they're indignant at someone trying to force them into a situation they haven't orchestrated."

"Oh, you're such a philosopher," Edgar laughed. "No, I think they're just scared. Come on, grab the vaccine. Let's get the pigs done."

We walked into the barn where Mr. Conley and his oldest daughter were hovering over a wooden box in a corner of the tack room. We said good morning, and Edgar began drawing the vaccines into the syringes.

The sound of rustling straw emanated from the wooden box—baby pigs, no doubt.

"Does it make any difference which of the pigs we do first, Doc?" Jim Conley said as he stepped over the partition and into the box. There was a scuffling, and then I heard low chirping noises coming from the enclosure. Mr. Conley reached inside to calm the little animals. With that, a chorus of high-pitched screams hit the air, breaking the damp silence of the morning.

I had once seen a television factoid explaining that a jet engine blast has a decibel rating of 135. In comparison, a pig's scream has a rating of 133 decibels. I agreed with those findings as I winced at the ear-splitting shrieks. Edgar's warning words about pig hysteria repeated in my mind. Then, as quickly as they had begun, the cries ended. Curiosity getting the better of me, I slipped into the tack room and peered inside the babies' box. There, cuddled into a mass in a corner of the four-by-four-foot wooden pen, were nine or ten piglets, all combinations of black and white. So entwined were they with each other that I could not tell which pig the legs belonged to and which pig the tail belonged to. Everything was mixed up on the pile—like a Picasso painting. They huddled together, their tiny, wrinkled noses sniffing the air for danger.

"How beautiful!" I gasped, reaching toward them. When they saw my hands coming for them, squeals let loose from the box, and the mass of pigs ran, in unison, to the other corner half hidden by an overhead shelf. They cowered beneath the overhang, each frantically pawing its brothers and sisters in an effort to dig its way to the bottom (and safest) part of the pile.

Mr. Conley, straddling the box and reaching under the shelf to grab the first patient, said, "Say, do you like them? I have two males left. The rest of the litter is spoken for." At the sound of his voice, the pile of piglets raced with a united squeal to the opposite corner where they pushed themselves into another jumbled pile. The tiny, frightened eyes darted anxiously from me to their owner.

They were surprisingly fleet of foot for such young, solid porkers. Sleek and compact, the cylindrical animals gave no sense of preciousness or brittleness, unlike small kittens and puppies. They were speeding bullets with legs. The size of a soup can, they looked as densely packed, too. Those big, brown liquid eyes radiated their fear of predators, large or small. Their expressions bespoke abject fear of injury and death by most anything. Their headlong rush to the opposite end of the pen demonstrated their terror of larger, carnivorous beings such as myself. No doubt they were sizing me up for my ability to make scrapple out of them.

"It's okay, piggily wiggilies," I cooed, completely smitten by their miniature stature and vulnerability. I wanted to take each piglet into my arms and protect it against the mad vaccinator. But, instead, I tried to reassure them with words. I said, "The shot will only last a few seconds, and then you can go back to Mommy. We won't hurt you—just a little sting."

The pile of pigs stared uncomprehendingly at me. They readied themselves to run to the opposite corner.

"I am absolutely enthralled," I said. "Piglets are the contest winners of cute animal babies. Of course, Hazel out there is nice, too, but her features and size have grown out of their initial enchanting stage. She's still a pretty pig, Mr. Conley, but nothing like her babies."

Mr. Conley laughed and grabbed one of the pigs as they raced again in hog unit formation to the opposite corner. Caught helplessly in his grip, the one piglet revved his jet engine. In a microsecond it was screaming such a high-pitched sound that I thought for sure we would all be deaf for at least two weeks. It was louder and shriller and more piercing than any rock concert I had ever been to. Jim held onto the wriggling animal while it launched a horrendous, unabated attack on our ears. . . .

Mr. Conley's daughter, Katie, left us for a moment, then appeared in the doorway. "Hazel is trying to get into the barn to get to her babies. She is *really* upset. Do you hear her trying to break in?" she said. "I have everything locked tight."

I could faintly make out the sound of wood banging against wood—a persistent barrage. Katie ran out into the aisle, but it was too late. The hundred-pound mother pig had barreled with Schwarzenegger-like strength into one of the two barn doors—doors tall and wide enough to allow a tractor through—and knocked it off the hinges.

"Look out! Here she comes!" Katie shouted.

"Quick! Get into the box with me and the piglets," Jim yelled. "She can't get us there." Edgar and I hopped into the pen as Hazel, snorting and squealing with fury, plowed her way into the tack room.

The alarmed piglet had scrambled back to the camouflaged haven of its brothers and sisters. Temporarily, we lost it as it burrowed quietly into the black and white uniformity of the group. Immediately when her brood quieted, the mother calmed, too. Moments later, she was hunting for spilled grain, as docile as when we had seen her earlier.

"Here, Hazel. Here, Hazel," Katie called. Hazel answered, "Froo-oo-oom," turned, and sashayed off as calm as could be in Katie's direction. Edgar quickly jumped out of the box and barricaded the door to the tack room. Then I stepped over the partition and out of the box so that Edgar could administer the vaccines. While he injected one piglet, I readied the next one.

Jim snagged another piglet as the herd raced beneath the shelf. It was a male. The raucous squealing started again as

Mr. Conley held the pig's head against his chest, its back end exposed for the shot. Once again, Hazel began throwing herself against the door with motherly ferocity. Quickly, Edgar injected the piglet. Last, he ran a pink chalk mark down the pig's back to mark him.

What a racket the pig made—all over a silly shot. But to him it was hardly innocuous. His mouth gaped, opening and panting with every intake of breath and with every scream. I held my ears against the wailing, and at the same time, I also looked into his eyes. And what I saw wasn't necessarily fear. No. I was convinced he was not screaming out of cowardice. To the contrary. What I recognized in those crystal-brown eyes was nothing short of indignation. The piglet was staging conniptions, because we were violating his sense of dignity and self. He had not sanctioned this shot-giving ceremony. It was something that had been decided by someone else, another species no less. His fury was against our forcing him into something he wanted no part of.

This pig's loud protests were like the "frantic screams" of all the characters of modern literature beset by existential angst, that feeling of dread or death that forces the hero to sustain a sense of self. Those characters, like Saul Bellow's Henderson the Rain King, Joseph Heller's Yossarian, and Norman Mailer's protagonists, were all rebels, all radical innocents who were desperately trying to cling to a sense of self-determination amid a dehumanizing society. Similarly, this potbelly seemed to be yelling in his piggy voice, "No, no, no. I won't have it. I refuse categorically because I have not *chosen* to be immunized. I have not allowed you to lay a hand on me!" Indeed, the pig was a radical innocent—a pure, unadulterated being of the barnyard who, at the moment, was reacting hysterically and with much raucous objection to the taking away of his right to direct his future and act according to his personal needs.

In only a few seconds, Jim released the pig to the rest of the pack. Then he picked up the next one. I had already drawn up all the other vaccines and put them within Edgar's reach. But I had to leave—the noise was too deafening, and my sympathy for the little piglets too overwhelming.

"I told you pigs always scream like that," Edgar yelled after me as I fled, hands cupping my ears. "It will be all over in a few seconds anyway, Gay." I ran from the tack room, past Katie, who had locked a furious Hazel into a horse stall, out to the yard and into the truck.

I slammed the truck door to shut out their screams and misery. There were eight more pigs to be done. But even in the truck I could still hear the cries from the defenseless animals. I could imagine all that was happening by listening to the squeals. With the first sharp squeak there was the capture of another victim. Once the shrieks became continuous and panting, I envisioned Edgar rubbing the pig's rump with alcohol. Add a few seconds for him to reach for the syringe, in which time the squeal lowered a few decibels to 130, and then the highest shriek of all—the shot hitting home. The screams continued until Edgar had drawn the chalk line across his back. Then complete silence as the inoculated piglet was released into the pen. In the background, the mother wailed miserably.

After fifteen minutes of this commotion, there was dead quiet. The fog was starting to lift, and the horses in the field were calmly devouring their breakfast. Deciding that Edgar must have finished vaccinating all the pigs, I climbed down from the truck and stepped once again into the barn. Edgar was drying his hands with paper towels, and he and Jim were walking from the tack room, mission accomplished.

I peeked into the wooden box where the mass of piggies huddled, probably fearful I was going to do something else to them. Only a few weeks old, I thought, but so aware of their own helplessness and their loss of dignity. Eighteen little chocolate eyes stared with wary anticipation. I was immediately smitten. I could conquer those instinctive fears once the animal trusted me, I thought. A pig of my very own, I mused, would feel safe and protected in my arms. He would forget he was prey.

I walked over to Jim and Edgar.

"I want one," I said.

Edgar's eyes popped. Then they rolled with disapproval. "You already . . . "

I cut off his words. "I want a pig," I declared smiling. "Of the two males that are left, I want the tiniest—the runt."

"Step right over here, young lady, and take your pick," carnival Jim cajoled, putting his arm around my shoulder.

Edgar lingered behind as if by ignoring my enthusiasm it would disappear. He might have known that wouldn't work.

Jim stepped again into the box, and the pigs shrieked and darted beneath the shelf. Jim knew the pigs individually by their markings. He pointed out two piglets—one with a lot of chrome (white hair) around his neck and the other with a smaller collar. The one with the smaller collar was the runt of the litter. He looked up at me, and I looked at him. I was enamored by his rich, dark chocolate eyes. He didn't turn away as I bent down toward the box, just stared at me curiously. I was permanently enchanted, love-struck.

"That one!" I said, pointing at my piggy. The smallest pig

looked up at me, sniffing the air with his rubbery nose, and then he turned with a mini-snort and ran to the safety of the pack.

"Gay, you don't really want. . . . " Vaguely I heard Edgar's disapproval in the background.

"When can we pick him up?" I asked Jim.

"They'll be ready to go in another four weeks," Jim said.

"How much is he?"

"Fifty dollars."

"Deal," I said, my smile widening into a grin.

"Some deal," Edgar mumbled. He was shaking his head, hoping to dampen my resolution, but when I really want something, I am adamant. Looking at me, Edgar knew I was determined to have this pig.

Although Jim had encouraged me, I didn't need any prodding.

Jim went on to explain, "As I said before, they're a bit wild right now. They haven't been handled much, but if you spend time with your guy, he'll tame up nice for ya," Jim said. "Ya know, all my life I've been a dog person. My dog went with me wherever I went—to the racetrack, to the market, downtown, everywhere. Now don't get me wrong—I just love dogs. But, damn it, as far as I'm concerned, you can't beat a pig for a pet."

I looked at Edgar for a sign of weakness.

Jim continued, "Yep, I love pigs. They're so intelligent it's scary. Ours certainly can out-think me. Plus, they're ten times cleaner than any dog, and they're very affectionate. Hazel follows me around the farm all day—just has to be with me all the time."

"I don't know the first thing about keeping a pig," I admitted.

"Oh, there's nothing to it. You buy a little pig chow for his two daily meals. After he gets to know where home is, you'll be able to just let him loose, and he'll pick up scraps and graze in your yard. They are real easy keepers. Pigs are very territorial, so they won't wander away. They spend all day just rooting around the yard, searching for different things to eat. In fact, you probably won't have to feed him at all during the summer and fall. They find enough food around to live off entirely."

"See," I said to Edgar who was frowning, his passive method of disapproval. I knew this meant he had given ground and I smiled warmly at him. Edgar just shook his head. "It won't take any trouble to have a pig," I parroted Jim. "All you do is let him out into the yard, and he'll take care of himself."

"Yeah, right," Edgar said and sighed, obviously resigned.

"Sure, sure," said Jim. "It's true, Doc. You'll be glad you took him. They make wonderful pets. I promise you won't regret it. If you don't like him, I'll take him back."

"Well, I can't argue with those terms," Edgar said.

"I love him already!" I said, bursting with childlike excitement. "I can't wait to pick him up."

I took one more peek into the wooden box where the piglets huddled, but I couldn't recognize mine hidden amongst the rest of the camouflaged group. So I said goodbye to them all and climbed into the truck. Edgar pulled out of the driveway, and we headed toward the Poconos.

That afternoon, after lunch at Henri's, we stopped at the Crossings Outlet Mall in Tannersville to visit our friend Linda who had a shop there.

"Hey, Linda," I called, bursting through the revolving doors. "Guess what I got today?"

"Now what!" she giggled as she saw the telltale frown on Edgar's face.

"A Vietnamese potbellied pig!" I proudly exclaimed.

She looked incredulous. Then she turned with a grin to Edgar, who was rolling his eyes again. "A pig! A little piggy-wiggy?" she cooed in a high little girl's voice.

"Yes," I said proudly. "He's the cutest thing. Pigs are supposed to be very intelligent, and they're no bother at all to keep. After he gets accustomed to his new home, all you do is let him loose, and he will hunt for his own food and stay right around the house. He won't roam like dogs do."

Linda's mouth hung open as I told her about our morning. Edgar wandered the story surveying the goods. After I finished, Linda offered no comment for quite awhile, and for just a moment I thought I'd better be prepared to accept some motherly advice to the tune of, *You really don't need another animal.*

But I was wrong.

After a few silent moments, Linda said, "I want one, too!"

I was struck speechless. Then I came to my senses.

"Great!" I said. "We'll call Jim when we get to the truck. He's got just one more left. I'm telling you—they're going like hot cakes! We're so lucky to have gotten one before they were all adopted!"

Edgar came out of the shoe department and noticed our enthusiasm. "What are you two conjuring?" he asked suspiciously.

"Linda's getting the other pig!" I squealed with delight. "She's getting Lowell's brother!"

"Lowell?" Linda said. "You named him *Lowell*?"

"Yes, I was thinking about what I would name him on the way up here. That's a pretty unique name for a pig, isn't it? A boy I went to elementary school with had the name Lowell, and I always thought it so distinctive. I especially like the mellow notes in the name. You should see my little pig, Linda. He has such beautiful eyes."

Edgar was rolling his eyes again.

I pressed my hands together. "Yes, I was thinking about calling him either *Lowell* or *Lyle.* I finally decided on Lowell."

"Then my pig will be named Lyle," Linda said happily.

"Great! Lowell and Lyle—the two pig brothers."

"What's Jack going to say?" Edgar asked with an eyebrow raised. I knew what he was thinking: his own wife might be a lost cause, but he could save his fellow man, Jack, by deterring Linda from going down the same path.

"What's he going to say?" Linda said, hands on hips. "He's not going to say anything! If I want a pig, I am going to have one. My husband's got nothing to do with it. Whenever he wants something, he goes out and gets it. He never asks me if he can get those things, so why do I need to ask him?"

She and I slapped a high five—a signature of unity and triumph. Our determination to own pigs made us feel like low-key feminists in a man's world.

"Lowell and Lyle," Edgar said, sighing as he followed me through the revolving doors to the outside.

"Yep, isn't it great?" I laughed. "Isn't it great Linda is taking one, too? Our pigs can visit each other during the summer when school is out, and they can go camping together. And when I am busy, Linda will pig-sit Lowell, and I will sit for Lyle. The pig brothers can always stay in touch and visit each other; we can have *pignics*—get it? Oh, I can just see them playing and roughhousing by the pool while you cook the burgers over the grill and I get the drinks for the four of us." I skipped down the pavement toward the truck.

"Yeah. Jack, I'm sure, will be simply overjoyed."

I quietly ignored Edgar's dampening remark, figuring Lowell and I would eventually win him over. Glancing over my shoulder, I saw Linda waving from the store's big window. The smile on her face was nearly as broad as the one on my own.

In mid-November, when the pigs were nine weeks old, we picked up Lowell and Lyle. Edgar and I had put a few old rags in the cat carrier, in which we planned to transport the piglets. I was surprised to see they were twice as big as when I first saw them the day of their vaccinations. Putting them in the carrier was like trying to fit two gigantic loaves of pumpernickel into a standard bread box, but somehow we managed.

I was astonished they didn't complain about being confined in the cat carrier, but I soon discovered why they were fairly content in that confining box. They had the nearness of each other for comfort. This revelation would serve me well in sadder times, in times when I felt miserable, depressed, or threatened.

It all boiled down to a matter of *presence,* a feature I was to learn more of later on in my relationship with Lowell.

When we got home, Edgar and I set the cat carrier inside our newly renovated pen. We opened the carrier door, and with a little push the piggies darted onto the straw. Voicing little yelps of curiosity, they inspected every inch of their new home: the food dishes, the water dish, the litter pan. I reached in to touch them, but they shrieked in unison and fled in a heap to a corner. I hadn't touched either of them yet, and I was dying to. But the nine-inch, tubular shaped piglets were quite wild as Jim Conley had warned, and they needed to get used to the human touch.

They hunkered down in the corner as I reached to straighten out their blankets. Then suddenly, as if one had whispered to the other, *Let's go!* they both ran to the opposite end of the pen and again crouched in a pile. The little pigs were gorgeous, with glossy black coats, white collars and legs. *What substantial creatures,* I thought—so fully packed, so solid. I longed to hold one in my arms, but could see that wouldn't happen for a while. For now, I would just have to be content watching them.

It was amazing how the pig brothers did nearly everything together. They slept and breathed in unison, their chests rising and falling in harmony. Likewise, they awoke at the same instant and grunted simultaneously, as if their brains were linked by a modem. When I spoke to them, they answered together with little piggily noises whose meanings I had yet to decipher. Only much later would I come to understand a pig's language— quite a repertoire of messages, in fact. When they were scared, they reacted with a conjoined alarm and ran as one body to the far corner of the pen. The two pigs were as synchronized as schooling fish that dart and turn en masse. There almost seemed to be some kind of clairvoyant, prescient connection between them. Each mimicked the other's reaction, and each mirrored the other in action. As well, each depended on the other's presence for emotional support.

My plan was to tame them with tenderness and time. As yet untouched by feminine, human hands, the baby pigs were at first suspicious of my attempts to pet them. They had reason to be. Previously, they had only been handled by Jim Conley, who raised them, and by Edgar the Vet, who stuck injections under their skin and administered nasty de-worming medicine. It had been touch on demand, not by permission.

It took me many sittings, and numerous bribes of grapes and pieces of apple, to begin to allay their fear of people. Having trained and conditioned horses, I felt fairly confident as a therapist for pigs. After they grew accustomed to their new pen, I began my Training-Toward-Taming Program. One day, armed with a cup of slivered grapes, I climbed into the pen, ducked under the heating lamp, and sat down in the straw next to them. The porkers, startled from their morning nap, squealed with terror as this rather large person positioned herself in the middle of their territory. They darted to the far end of the pen, scrambling over each other, and eyed me suspiciously. I cooed in baby talk, but they were too scared to listen. Slowly, I extended my arm and offered a piece of grape.

The tiny rubbery noses twitched and sniffed the air. They smelled the grape dangling from my fingertips. Lowell, my pig of little chrome, began to make cute, little gurgling noises. He was interested in the grapes, but he was not yet brave enough to abandon the safety of his brother. I leaned closer, offering the fruit until Lowell moved one foot forward. Then I said in a low, soothing voice, "Good boy, Lowell," and lay the grape on the straw in front of him.

Lowell looked at me suspiciously, moved another step closer to the grape and nudged it. After smelling it and deciding that it was, indeed, edible and therefore not likely to attack, he rolled the grape over with his nose and lapped it into his mouth. Quickly he chewed the grape, his lips smacking, his tongue licking, mixing the fruit with the air to savor the taste. I smiled at his open-mouthed chewing and the wet, delicious munching noises. Soon Lowell's sucking sounds drew Lyle's attention. I put another grape down for Lyle. He eyed it, stole stealthily toward it, and lapped the fruit into his mouth. Then he ran back to his corner where he could safely enjoy the grape, his lips smacking as loudly as Lowell's.

It took only ten minutes to persuade the pigs to accept

grape morsels from my hand, although they still darted to the corner if I tried to touch them. My strange voice and sizeable presence were obviously enough trauma for them.

With daily sessions like this, it took approximately four days until I was able to gain their confidence enough that they would allow me to pat their heads. The next step in the conditioning process was to withhold a portion of grape until each piglet had allowed me to touch an ear, ever so lightly and quickly. Once allowed a tweak, I offered a sliver of grape as a reward. In this way, they conditioned me, too, for they knew that to get food from me, all they needed to do was hold still for a pat. In a short time, they reasoned it was no skin off their hides to let me touch them, plus they would get goodies for the effort.

By the fifth day, they were all over me when I came into the pen. To them I was the swine angel, the bearer of juicy, delectable treats. I was the Santa Claus of the porcine set, with her full red cheeks, her belly laugh, and her large sack of fruit snacks. I brought raisins, tiny bits of apple, pieces of carrot (which, I discovered, were too hard for their baby teeth to chew) and cut-up cranberries for Thanksgiving. When I climbed into their pen, the two piglet brothers seemed to become a ravenous mob, squealing, not out of fear anymore, but out of curiosity for a new and interesting snack. It was not too long before they figured out this human was not a predator, but a vending machine that would spit treats on request.

Once I could pet the little pigs while feeding them goodies, the next step was to persuade them to crawl into my lap and accustom Lowell and Lyle to being held. Sitting in the straw, I lured them with goodies to my side, and when they accidentally put a foot on my thigh, their reward was a piece of apple or such. It wasn't long before both of them were jumping into my lap. Then, while they were absorbed in eating, I gradually encircled them with my arm, touching them very lightly around their bodies. When they discovered the prolonged touch didn't hurt and, in addition, resulted in a treat, they soon tolerated my arm around them for an extended time. It wasn't long before I was able to hold, in my lap, each pig while he happily lapped up the treats.

Part of their learning experience also had to do with table manners—something they lacked. Lowell was the more aggressive of the two pigs. In order for Lyle to get his share of the feast, I had to temper Lowell's snap-mouthy enthusiasm. They were in competition with each other over the grape pieces, but by the time I had completed their lessons, the baby pigs had learned to patiently wait their turn for the next handout. But this forbearance, in Lowell's case, didn't last long. Lowell soon became so trusting of me that he began snatching the fruit with a terrible vengeance. Like a shark in a feeding frenzy, he leaped like a missile for the goody to which I was attached. Make no mistake: piggy bites hurt, even from pigs only a couple of months old. So, after a few raps on the nose accompanied by, "No, don't bite Mommy," Lowell learned to restrain his excitement. Thereafter, he took the morsels from my fingers like a proper gentlepig. To this day he accepts my treats more daintily than if Miss Manners herself had taught him!

After these taming sessions, the piglets and I reached a turning point, during which Lowell stopped running into a corner with the treat still dangling from his mouth and instead let me stroke him repeatedly as he ate. Then, during a very special moment, our relationship became even more solid. In one grand gesture, which succeeded in enamoring him to me forever, Lowell stood firmly and without trepidation and allowed me to touch his quarter-sized snout. For my young sophisticate of the porcine set, this was an act of supreme compromise, for Lowell's snout was his *raison d'être*.

To understand the pig's nose is to understand the animal himself. First, a pig's snout is an *objet d'humeur*. No other animal's schnozzle resembles it or seems to have a life of its own as does that of the swine. It is, in reality, an entity unto itself. From the very beginning, I was enamored with the object that he was always careful to protect from my touch—his own symbol of virginity.

During the first "untouchable" days when I could only sit observing him in the clean straw of his pigpen, I inspected that snout minutely. After a few days of observation, I was hopelessly obsessed with it. Was it soft and mushy to the touch? It always looked wet, except when he was sleeping, so I wondered if it was slimy-wet or just smooth-wet. Where did the rather large and tunnel-like nostrils lead, and how, I thought scientifically, might it look in cross-section? Could the proboscis that resembled an electrical outlet really plug into smells with more expertise and finesse than the nose of a dog, or was it all just "show"? I imagined Lowell's smeller at work, rooting through the horse manure pile for scraps of grain, tunneling through the sawdust bin for tasty insects, and when he got old enough to leave the barn, plowing the ground for grubs and worms and digging through every other tantalizing, food-filled area on our farm. I concluded that his nozzle and his breath must have a perennially foul odor. Then I agonized over the nose's seeming elasticity, its tiny sweat pores, its strength, and its incessant and tireless energy.

Perhaps, most of all, I fathomed what warped humorist

designed the potbellied pig and its snoot. Thus far, I had pretty much figured that it had to have been engineered by a caricaturist of sorts—the same goddess responsible for conjuring other curious creatures such as armadillos, anteaters, and aardvarks.

After two weeks of taming sessions, when the moment of Lowell's grand gesture finally arrived, I was in virtual "pig heaven." In a moment of supreme self-abnegation, Lowell proffered his snout for me to touch. It was the penultimate gesture of faith and confidence, and in one great synthesizing moment all my questions were finally answered. Upon the delectable second when he allowed me to tweak the tip of it, I discovered a "watery-wet," rubber-hard appendage that, despite all its poking and prodding into, around, and through unsavory areas of the outdoors, did not have *any* bad odor at all. In fact, if anything, it smelled earthy-sweet.

One might wonder how I came close enough to detect the fragrances of Lowell's snout. With no offer of apology, I divulge a secret. I knelt in the straw before him in a position of abject selflessness and reverential awe. I faced him on his level—on the ground, head on. As I crawled toward him, Lowell's nozzle twitched and sniffed, and slowly, very stealthily, I touched my nose to his. The moment was electric. I felt accepted, as if I had been initiated into an elite group. It was a meeting of kindred souls, and it was the moment that sealed our friendship and solidified our trust in each other. We were, after that, two different entities united by a touch—a touch of curiosity, which became, as time went on, familiarity, acceptance, and finally love. We had bonded.

When I touched my nose to his, Lowell responded by working my schnozzle curiously, sniffing and manipulating mine much as a baker kneads a clump of dough. I held still while his nose pushed and prodded mine, wiggling mine from side to side, from left to right and from right to left. All the while, I could feel his nose exhaling, its warm breath caressing my cheeks. Though our two noses touched, I had yet to realize just what the appendage would feel like under my fingers. So, I reached out to touch his snout. The tip of Lowell's nose, like an upside-down V, slanted forward and pushed my palm, probing and inspecting it for edibility. Once it found my hand wasn't food, however, it assessed my fingers for danger. In an instant, the wriggling, probing snout determined me an ally, not an enemy—one with a soothing touch.

The snout approved me. I was joyous! I offered Lowell a slice of grape which he graciously and delicately accepted. In turn, Lowell offered me another touch to his nose—my reward. I was delirious with happiness: my pig trusted me. From then on, the sessions were repeated: a grape morsel in exchange for a nudge on the nozzle. The scene probably looked a bit bizarre, but no one was watching, so I didn't care. And I wouldn't have cared if anyone *had* seen as, each time, Lowell stood before me mesmerized, for several minutes.

One day when Lowell felt completely at ease, I began to delicately trace the contours of his nose: across the top, outlining the outer edge, circling the nostrils in a figure eight, up to the V point again, and around the edge for a second trip. Slowly, deliberately, I caressed his nose, tracing the unique design. Lowell's eyes closed, and I yawned, both of us tranquilized by my hand's slow, repetitive movement. Soon my eyelids felt heavy, and I lay down in the clean straw in front of him.

I was nearly asleep but continued to stroke his nose with a rhythmical, circling motion. Around the top, over the edge, around each hole, I traced a soft path. Repeatedly I outlined the schnozzle, a gesture not unlike a mantra.

Suddenly, Lowell dropped to the ground. I woke up with a start and sat upright. My pig lay motionless in the straw, his belly pointing skyward. My hands flew to my mouth. What had I done? Had I somehow hurt him? He lay on his side like a dead thing, his naked underside exposed, his legs stiffened at right angles to his body, his toes pointed.

"Lowell?" I whispered, my voice catching in my throat. "Lowell, are you okay?"

I hovered over him and saw one eye open, regarding me intensely. He lay prostrate, as rigid as an iron bar, in the straw. I stared for what seemed moments, then suddenly I noticed movement in his rib cage. Thank goodness my fallen angel was still alive. I sighed with relief as his chest rose and fell rhythmically. "Good," I whispered aloud, "he's still breathing." Later on I would realize that I had literally hypnotized him by repetitive stroking, and he had collapsed out of complete relaxation. My catatonic animal lay overcome, breathing slowly and nodding his head as if to say, *Go ahead, keep up the massage. Don't stop now.*

So I rubbed the great expanse of belly, so hairless and velvety soft. I had once read that exposing the abdomen was the ultimate statement of trust from a pig. After all, for all Lowell knew, I could have been a butcher eyeing that vulnerable expanse for cold cuts. Or I could have been a football player coveting the ball that might have been. Instead, my pig put his confidence in my soothing, quiet fingers. I stroked him softly, whispering sweet things, and eased myself back into the straw.

Yet, as much as I felt certain he had collapsed out of complete relaxation, his body position, stiff as a flat rock, was anything but relaxed. In fact, he could just as easily have been composed of concrete as of malleable tissue and fluids. He was a surreal portrait of rigid contentment. I laughed softly at the sight.

Then Lowell yawned, and as I continued to scratch his underbelly, he began to direct my efforts by lifting his hind leg and pointing it skyward, like a ballerina. He lifted his thigh higher so that I should not miss a spot. I rubbed diligently. Then he wriggled onto his back, his front legs folded across his chest, a grin on his face. His exposed stomach begged for more. So, giggling under my breath (I couldn't let him see my amusement), I massaged between his front legs, his back legs, and swirled my hand all along his tummy. At this point I could have done almost anything to him; he lay completely oblivious to the real world—in sheer tummy-rubbing intoxication.

While I continued to stroke him, I pondered the nature of such a beast that would throw itself to the ground in hypno-tized euphoria. His drop to the floor was so abrupt, so deliber-ate—like Drew Carey on his television show, falling from his roof as his friends watched. But, unlike that character, Lowell fell over not out of clumsiness, but out of ecstacy.

From that time on, I could always elicit that same reaction just by lightly rubbing Lowell's side—the promise of a union between human and swine to come. Through the late fall and early winter, the scenario remained the same: *Rub, rub, scratch, scratch, swirl.* Then, *SLAM!* when Lowell dropped to the ground. All the while, the up-side eye scrutinized me, de-manding I continue the rubbing, which I gladly did, barely able to contain my laughter. By habit, he came to expect his mas-sages to last at least fifteen minutes, about the time it took my fingers to become numb.

My final order of business was to train Lowell to a harness. Slippery pigs are just that—elusive and uncatchable. Should my wonderful, new pet escape me without wearing a harness, I would be lucky to ever get him back. He could just gallop into the woods, never to be heard from again. Up until this time, I had Lowell and Lyle caged in a small pen. I kept them in the pen except for the occasional stroll around the tightly sealed barn. Although the two piggies didn't realize it, their confinement was synonymous with their safety. Even with Lyle going home to Linda and Jack in a few days and Lowell getting their pen all to himself, I knew he would outgrow the small house in time. So, the sooner he became accustomed to a harness and being outside of his pen, the better off both he and I would be.

When I slipped the harness with relative ease over Lowell's head and buckled it over his back, I foolishly thought everything would go smoothly and with little effort. Next, I attached one of the horse's lead ropes to the harness and lifted a seemingly unperturbed Lowell out of his small pen. I carried Lowell into the indoor riding arena, then put him down.

Feeling the constricting harness around his neck and belly, Lowell immediately rebelled. He took off like a fox from the hunt in what appeared to be an effort to run right out of the harness. Desperately clinging to the other end of the lead, I ran behind Lowell, but I could hardly keep up with the wily pig who raced along the path in the indoor arena like a greyhound. Suddenly, a huffing and puffing Lowell jerked to a stop. His eyes darted anxiously around, no doubt hoping to find an escape from the harness. I tried to offer soothing words to my pig friend, but could only cough and gasp for air after the sudden and unexpected race. With an abrupt squeal of protest, Lowell was off again, a tiny missile screaming around the track.

Lowell's energy was endless. Several times we rounded the track together. Sometimes he went a little slower allowing me to jog, and other times he went as fast as his little legs could carry him, forcing me into a full run. I could almost see the wheels turning in his head; for sure, he thought, he could outrun this agitating constriction around his belly, and the human shadow that trailed his every move.

In time Lowell slowed, allowing me to catch my breath. Even though he didn't look very pleased, he accepted that he couldn't get rid of the weight and confining feel of the harness. Then I quickly went to work, conditioning him to come to me when I tugged on the lead rope. When I first gave him a verbal command along with a tug that pulled him toward me, he gave me a wary and annoyed look and refused to budge, obviously still upset about the harness. But I didn't give up. I calmly explained to him the need for this lesson and promised him that the sooner he cooperated, the sooner he could shed the harness. When I tried a second time, he reluctantly took a step closer to me, which resulted in a grape. I again asked him to "come" while simultaneously pulling on the rope. He tripped forward, and I offered another grape. In a matter of minutes Lowell was harness trained. I was then able to take the lead rope off and teach him to come when called. I was soon able to walk away from him, utter the word "come," and he would sidle obediently to my side, his little tail wagging. Never before had I had such a fast learner as a pet. All other animals I had ever kept were comparatively slow and reluctant to be trained. The horses needed endless conditioning and repetition and although dogs were better, they still took time. I was discovering that training pigs was relatively easy and rewarding. While they might react a bit hysterically at first, their reasoning powers soon take over, and they soak up information like children.

After I had tamed Lyle in like fashion, we delivered him to his new home in the Poconos where he would live with Linda and Jack and their three horses. It was hard giving Lyle up, and I had to remind myself that Lyle had never been mine to begin with. Like Lowell, Lyle, was also a sucker for a rub on the belly. I guess that's partially what made it so hard for me to take him to his new home: he reminded me so much of Lowell. But Lyle, I told myself, would have just as nice a home as Lowell had and lots of other animals to keep him company, too. And I promised to visit him often.

Those first weeks with Lowell and Lyle, and even after Lyle left, amazed and amused me. I had to laugh quietly and to myself though, so that Lowell wouldn't hear or see my giggles. I laughed at the incongruity, the surrealism of owning such a pet. I found that though Lowell was plump, he was swift and fleet of foot. While he was quick to hysteria, he was reasonable and calm in the end. Though he was cautious, once he trusted, he was fearless. Despite a reputation for being a filthy type of animal, Lowell was fastidious about keeping neat and clean. And as "out of it" or "unaware" as he and his relatives appeared to some, he proved to be quick-witted and alert as a fox and as attentive and vigilant as a guard dog. While some people thought he surely could not show the affection of more traditional pets, his desire to touch me and draw me near proved them wrong. He had no command of the English language, yet I came to understand his verbalizations and body language as well as I understood my husband's.

Most incongruous in a pig is its humanity; when I see Lowell delight in good conversation or a cozy nap, I recognize something of myself. A pig is so human in intelligence, in appetite, in personality, in motivation, in desires that in many ways, which I discovered through time spent with my pet, the pig is psychologically human. And it is this incongruity, this surreal quality that is the essence of the pig, as well as the foibles and quirks of human nature seen in the animal, that make him such a humorous creature. I've learned that when we find comedy in the pig's personality and character, we are, in a way, laughing at ourselves.

There are many who view a pig's physique as a source of humor. I saw Lowell's shape as delightful and pleasing to the eye. He was the epitome of round—all circles and plumpness. He had a round rump, round belly, circular jowls, rounded ears, spherical nose. A more curvaceous animal I had yet to meet. Though some people regard a pig as an ugly animal, from an artist's perspective and mine, he is as beautiful, as round and fully packed as one of Renoir's bathers. Often, I stood nearby contemplating his physique, as though appreciating a sculpture in a museum. Lowell was a truly sensual creature—an artistic delight.

While I learned a lot about my pig friend in those first months, I discovered a great deal about myself, too. A very valuable lesson was the ability to appreciate the simpler pleasures in life as Lowell did. I learned to savor every bite of food and relish it to the last crumb. In fact, from Lowell I learned to taste my food first before gobbling it up. Lowell was never so quick to get his dinner in his stomach that he neglected to savor the flavor. Each bite was deliberate, mused upon, and contemplated. Lowell did not eat like hogs have been mythologized to eat; he ate appreciatively, pensively, like a gourmand sampling the finest repast.

I also learned to appreciate the importance of touch with

regard to all my animals and my human friends, too. Though I'm not the real "touchy-kissy" type, even now, I have somewhat broadened my horizons in that area. Certainly I don't give a massage to all I meet, but a handshake or a pat on the shoulder goes a long way toward gaining people's trust and friendship.

Another important lesson learned from Lowell was to be wary of strangers and to only give my trust when it has been earned. From his point of view, living in a world of butchers and hotdog eaters, such an attitude is necessary for his survival. While I don't have the same worries or fears as my dear pig, I have come to appreciate this lesson as valuable to my own well-being, and it has led me to recognize the importance of listening to, trusting, and acting upon my instincts.

The most important lesson Lowell taught me, however, was to enjoy the humor in everyday situations. I began to see that one should be more aware and more perceptive of the funny things that animals do and that is revealed through the careful observation of wildlife. In life's more humorous moments, people become more accepting of others, more able to laugh than criticize. More than anything else, my humorous pig taught me to chuckle when the road gets a little rough. And when the road becomes unnavigable, he conveyed through his acts that I should fight with a vengeance and find my own way.

from LOWELL

Props

RAYMOND LEE

$\mathcal{H}$e was found whimpering one rainy morning in a clothes basket by Bill Buskirk, head of the Property Department, the genial stage boss of the Fine Arts Studio in Hollywood. Bill called his find Props, and all hands promptly adopted the puppy as their mascot. But not for long. Soon everyone from D. W. Griffith on down was seeking the favor of the brown-eyed foundling and he was given the run of the lot.

As the 1915 epics unreeled Props displayed a quite remarkable intelligence and understanding. Some other dog might have just nosed around the film factory. Not Props. He must have realized how much he was needed. Mapping out a schedule like all other movie people working under the Fine Arts banner, he never was off an hour in his routine, except when acting before the cameras himself.

Every morning the little dog met Dad Thoren, the gateman, as he opened the studio to traffic. He gave a wagging, individual greeting to both the walking and riding personnel. Dad swore he could tell time because at nine o'clock sharp Props would always tail off for his morning tour of the companies in production.

He would watch a scene or two being shot, receive a pat on the head or a mouth-watering sweet, and then he'd go on to the next stage. As the companies broke for lunch he'd sit outside the little bungalow-cafe where the actors and crew ate. No dog had ever eaten so well no matter how big his salary.

His after-lunch siesta always took place in the confines of the Property Department. He paid special tribute to Bill Buskirk by snoozing under his desk.

Oftentimes the prop hands would play a quick game of poker or roll the dice following their lunch. And on occasion, a snooping "efficiency expert," an unexplained agent who tried to save money for the studio, while making an inspection tour would catch and reprimand them. Second offenders were sometimes fired.

But this was B.P.—Before Props. When a game started, Props would suddenly unwind himself from his siesta and park outside the building, seeming to resume his snooze. After a while the boys heard a growl; then a bark; then a series of barks. Curious, a player would sneak a look out front. Ducking back inside, his whispered warning would break up the game. Props was giving the old heave-ho to an efficiency expert.

How the little spotter ever took up this guard duty nobody could ever imagine, but Props never failed his post and not a hand ever got the axe for flirting with Lady Luck on studio time.

I always remember a big moment at Miss Sarah P. McClung's school for us Triangle Kiddies. As school let out Props would always be there with a jumping, kissing greeting and a begging for some playtime. This lasted about ten minutes, after which he would hightail it for the stages again. No matter how we coaxed he never would play more than ten minutes.

At the end of the day he waited outside the projection room where the rushes, the day's shooting, were run off. Sometimes a director who favored him, like Paul Powell, would take him in and he'd watch the screen as attentive as any human.

No one knew where Props slept. He could be discovered in a variety of spots: One time he'd be in a luxurious bed used in a Bessie Barriscale society drama, another time in the dressing room of Dorothy Gish, who taught him many of his amazing tricks. Once Griffith found him curled up in his favorite office chair. As a bevy of assistants waited for an explosion, D. W., father of films, just smiled and patted Prop's head and sat in another chair.

How Props entered pictures was almost as story-book as his appearance in the clothes basket.

The Triangle Kiddies, of which I was now a Junior member, were working with beautiful Norma Talmadge in *Children in the House.* Props, paying his daily visit, just sat watching. Baby Charles Spofford had a big scene coming up. At two years Baby Charles could act the pants off of any of us.

In the scene with Baby Charles we plop him into a wagon to get rid of him. As we wander off he falls asleep. Suddenly as he shifts the wagon starts rolling toward a nearby gully. Norma Talmadge enters just in time to rescue him.

On direction from Christy Cabanne, the scene progressed. We put Baby Charles in the wagon, he closed his eyes, the prop men started pulling the wires attached to the wagon. The wagon moved slowly downhill. But just as Miss Talmadge entered she tripped and fell over a tree branch. Everyone froze. The wagon hit a rock, broke loose from the wires, headed for the gully. Props suddenly dashed from behind the camera and flung himself in front of the wagon. It stopped inches short of the gully.

As Mrs. Grover held her priceless Baby Charles in her arms,

hero Props licked away his tears and won himself a career. Fortunately, cameraman Frank Good had kept grinding and the exciting action was on film.

Props, while viewing the rushes, was jumping up and down barking like he didn't recognize himself but later, when Christy Cabanne explained it was himself, the little dog sat quiet and watched a rerun.

There was no stopping Props now. Everyone wanted him for a picture. And no one had to pay a dime for his services! A truly unique setup in high-salaried Hollywood.

He ran the gamut of emotions from comedy to tragedy with such top box-office winners as DeWolfe Hopper, of stage fame, in his first film, *Casey At the Bat;* the Gish sisters; H. B. Warner in some cloak and dagger thrillers; and he was once loaned to William S. Hart for a shoot-em-upper.

But his greatest role everyone agreed was in a Dorothy Gish classic called, *The Little Yank.* George Siegmann, remembered for his villainy in Griffith's *Birth of a Nation,* directed. It was quite common in the early days for actors to do several chores, thus revealing their multiple talents.

The story had a Civil War background. Siegmann wanted to show some of the pathos Griffith always incorporated in his films. He tried several ideas and then sat down for a conference.

Props was sitting on Dorothy Gish's lap eating peanuts. Suddenly she jumped up and peanuts and Props fell every which way. She rushed over to her director and explained her inspiration. Siegmann shrugged his shoulders. At this point he'd try anything. Anything was to be Props.

The scene took place on a Southern battlefield. The hero, Elmer Clifton, later the director who discovered Clara Bow, shoots at what he thinks is another soldier hiding behind a bush. It turns out to be a dog—Props. He is so overcome with humiliation and pity he makes a splint for the dog's leg and hides him from further harm on the explosive countryside.

Impressed with the canine's natural talent, Siegmann called for a close-up as Props first tried to walk on his splint. Sniffles, tears and applause, plus kisses showered by Dorothy, crowned the foundling's acting. Following this performance Siegmann naturally built up Prop's part.

from NOT SO DUMB

Sharing the Pain

NANCY B. GIBBS

As we awoke that gloomy summer morning, I felt a strong sense of dread. Going to the dentist was not one of my favorite activities to wake up to, but the days when I was forced to take my twin sons for any type of medical or dental treatments mark some of the worst days of my life. As much as I dislike going myself, I'd trade places with them anytime.

The day turned out worse than I could have imagined. Between the two boys, they had eight wisdom teeth removed. Having two twenty-year-old young men moaning at the same time was not my idea of having fun. They were miserable as the dentist packed their mouths with white gauze.

After the procedure was completed and we received the dentist's instructions, we left his office for home. It took both my husband and me to get the boys into the car and then inside the house.

Following the dentist's instructions, the boys sat up in the recliners, which were side by side in our living room. The moaning didn't cease as their pain seemed to fill every corner of the room. Strips of gauze were sticking out of both of their mouths.

Daisey, our five-pound toy poodle, had compassion for the boys when she heard them groaning. For a while, she stood and stared at them with her tail tucked. She was very quiet.

When she turned to look at me, sadness filled her eyes. For a long time we both stayed right beside the boys, just in case they had a need.

A little while later, Daisey disappeared. It was very unusual for her to leave the room where I was. She's never very far from her master and best friend. I decided that she couldn't stand seeing the boys so sick, so she slipped off into another room to grieve.

Just a few minutes later, to our surprise, Daisey returned to the living room. She firmly held a white sock in her mouth. She stared at the boys while holding on to it. Then she lay down on the floor facing them. She continuously cut her eyes from one of the boys to the other. Daisey knew that there wasn't much she could do, but decided that she could share in the pain with them. After the bleeding stopped and the boys removed the gauze, Daisey retired her sock, as well. It was soaking wet.

Many times when someone close to us experiences difficulties and hardships, we are not sure what we can do to help. Daisey taught me that day that we may not be able to correct every problem, but with God's help, we can most definitely share in the pain. Lending an ear, offering a hug or just being there can ease many burdens. Just as Daisey's compassion made the boys smile, our presence and concern can bring smiles to the ailing, as well.

When the boys started feeling better, Daisey jumped from one chair to the other, wagging her tail while gently licking their faces. I'm not sure who was happier when a glimmer of hope returned to the room that day—Daisey or me.

Blue Days and Blue Jays

JAIME JACOBS

I hadn't been myself lately . . . I was a little low, a little slow. One of the usual remedies, going to the garden, had been difficult to accomplish, for various reasons. Thus it was with a surge of relief that I was finally able to spend some moments in the yard. It was difficult to be depressed while working the soil, planting seeds, amending earth, sweeping, raking, piling rocks and collecting pine cones. It was especially hard because spring was on the way.

The air was damp, the breeze unsubtle and chill, watering my eyes and stiffening my hands. I didn't mind the discomfort because it served to remind me how alive, how sensate, I was in spite of myself. My other senses were rewarded in a wonder of ways, like my clothes redolent with rosemary and peppermint after brushing against those bushes, and the quirking cantata of crows next door. I saw so many pleasing sights, the reddish ruffles of new rose leaves, the blooms of baby scarlet flax on waifish stems, like perfect drops of blood suspended in mid-air . . . the wriggle of worms seeking to regain their depth after a breathy upheaval by my trowel.

I was conscious of my audience—the wary surveillance of sparrows and the soft gossip of mourning doves worried by my ministrations with the mulch. But my most ardent observers had to be a pair of blue jays, male and female, who seemed to be everywhere at once. In the early mornings, they would be on the back fence with full beaks, later they harangued finches at the bird bath or chased each other in the cypresses. When I went outside they followed my progress through the yard, sometimes coming quite close to see, and possibly to be seen, for they were handsome birds. The female was large, with colors of buff and beech, beige and black and sky-blue, while her partner was larger still and brighter. His was the blue of picturebooks and summer seaside postcards. Their eyes were big and had a picaresque gleam.

While I worked I found myself attuned to their movements, enjoying their enjoyment of the day. By turns they lurked, they launched themselves from place to place, they seemed to laugh outright, their busy-ness a result of birdish inquisitive-ness and, as it turned out, eager anticipation. Once, the female landed in a hanging basket over my head, surprising me with her balance as the pot swung crazily askew.

They provided a happy background as I pushed seeds into the soil, such a hopeful enterprise. Forget-me-nots, salvia, catnip, basil, sweet William, nasturtium, morning glory . . . dreaming of future color, future scent, the butterflies to come . . . little life-germs coming awake, and quickening my heart in the process.

When it grew too dark to continue, I wiped my hands in satisfaction and stretched my crinkled back. I snapped off a salute to my pair of partners and wished them good night.

Not long after, I looked out the window to get one last, albeit dusky, glimpse of my handiwork . . . and saw the blue jays gleefully digging up my nasturtium plot. I could only bow to such jaunty initiative.

An Angel Named Taffy

ANNE WATKINS

---

*T*affy is a mixed-breed mutt dressed in a long, thick reddish-blonde coat. She's a small dog whose hair streams out behind her like golden ripples of sunlight when she is racing at top speed. The love that shines from her expressive dark brown eyes melts my heart. And up until a few summers ago, she had always been a one-person dog. Mine.

To say that she was unfriendly would be an understatement. She was never mean to anybody, but she sure was standoffish. And as for Taffy and my daughter, Laura, forget it—it was sibling rivalry from Day One. Taffy wanted nothing to do with Laura, and Laura wanted nothing to do with her!

Then something happened that shattered our family. Laura's cousin was killed in a grinding traffic accident. She and Laura were closer than sisters, and best friends to boot. Laura was devastated.

After the funeral, my active, vivacious daughter withdrew into herself and became silent and pale. She refused to go out with friends and wouldn't even talk on the phone. She didn't eat at all and began spending long hours alone in her room. Her depression was frightening. I didn't know how to help her.

One day as I sat working at the computer in the living room, I heard a scratch at the front door and went to investigate. There stood Taffy on the porch mat, staring through the screen into the house.

"What is it, girl?" I asked. For the first time in her life, she ignored me! She leaned to one side to peer around me, then raised a shaggy paw to scratch the door again. Puzzled, I opened it a crack to pet her. She glanced up at me, dodged my hand and made as if to squeeze inside.

"No, girl," I said, and closed the door. She whined and pawed the screen again. "Crazy dog," I muttered.

Taffy maintained her vigil at the door. She whimpered and growled, paced back and forth, and from time to time pawed at the screen. Whenever I went to the door, she adamantly ignored me. Whatever she wanted, it definitely wasn't me!

Soon I heard Laura stirring around down the hall. Taffy, who had settled into an uneasy position on the doormat, sprang to her feet and began clawing the screen again. When Laura walked into the living room, Taffy yipped excitedly and danced from side to side. I glanced at Laura, who looked as confused as I felt. "What's wrong with her, Mom?" she asked.

"Beats me," I replied. "She's been acting weird all day."

I went to the door again. Impatiently, Taffy sidestepped so she could see around me. Her eyes were focused on Laura and she started to softly, insistently "talk" to her through the screen. I opened the door, expecting Taffy to do her usual thing—jump all over me and want to play. Instead, she streaked past me without so much as a friendly tail wag and bounded straight to Laura.

Laura had stretched out on the couch and Taffy sprang up beside her, did a half turn, then plopped down. She laid her head in Laura's lap and gently placed one paw on her arm. With her cold, wet nose, she nudged Laura's hand.

"Mom!" Laura exclaimed. She stroked Taffy's long silky coat. "Do you see this? She's never done this before!"

I stared in amazement as the small dog nuzzled Laura, then snuggled in beside her as if they were old friends. Taffy, who had never willingly let Laura touch her, was now insisting on full body contact.

As I watched my daughter caress Taffy's head and comb her fingers through the dog's hair, an expression crept across her pale, sad face that did my heart good. For the first time in days, Laura smiled.

Laura and Taffy cuddled on the sofa all afternoon. Taffy vocalized the whole time; growling, whining, and yipping in her insistent doggy style. Though she didn't speak in words we could understand, there was no mistaking her meaning.

The same expression was in the little dog's gaze that I had only seen before when she looked at me. Love shone from her eyes as she smiled up at Laura. She snuggled her shaggy little body against my daughter and encircled her bruised spirit with a blanket of love so real it was almost visible.

Do angels always appear in human form? I don't believe that for a minute. That summer, when Laura needed an angel the most, one came to her in the shape of a small, standoffish mixed-breed mutt named Taffy. And guess what? After all these years, Taffy is still Laura's best friend.

ACKNOWLEDGMENTS

(continued from page ii)

"Herman, a Special Gift," by Nicole Caughlin, is used by permission of the author.

"Something Magical" is from *Animals as Guides for the Soul,* by Susan Chernak McElroy. Copyright © 1998 by Susan Chernak McElroy. Published by The Ballantine Publishing Group, a division of Random House, Inc.

"Homer and Ann" is from *Colter,* by Rick Bass. Copyright © 2000 by Rick Bass. Published by Houghton Mifflin Company.

"The Ultimate Couch Pigtato," by Cynnde Nielsen and Ed Kostro, appeared in *PETS: Part of the Family,* January/February 2000.

"Return of the Ducks," by Ardith Clarke, appeared in *Guideposts,* March 1973.

"Wild Kingdom," by Paula Wilshe, is used by permission of the author.

"Business Partners," by Susan McCullough, appeared in *PETS: Part of the Family,* November/December 1999.

"Babe in the Woods," by Shari Smyth, appeared in *Guideposts,* January 2000.

"The Godsend," by Mark Luce, appeared in *Dog Fancy,* June 2000.

"Clare's Story," by Jan Rogers, is used by permission of the author.

"One" is from *Tears & Laughter,* by Gene Hill. Copyright © 1981 by Gene Hill. Published by Petersen Prints.

"Honey-Bun" is from *Honey-Bun,* by Anne Stockton, Copyright © 1999 Educare Press. Published by Educare Press.

"Lowell" is from *Lowell,* by Gay L. Balliet. Copyright © 2000 by Gay L. Balliet. Published by New Horizon Press.

"Props" is from *Not So Dumb,* by Raymond Lee. Copyright © 1970 by A. S. Barnes and Co., Inc. Published by Castle Books.

"Blue Days and Blue Jays," by Jaime Jacobs, is used by permission of the author.

AN INVITATION TO OUR READERS

If you would like to share a true story about an animal in your life, we invite you to send it to us. You can e-mail it to: ltta.tripod.com or mail it to LTTA, Box 214, East Greenville, PA 18041.

Some of the stories in this book came from Guideposts readers, just like you, and we welcome your participation in this inspiring series.

A Note From the Editors

This original Guideposts series was created by the Book and Inspirational Media Division of the company that publishes *Guideposts,* a monthly magazine filled with true stories of people's adventures in faith. *Guideposts* is available by subscription. All you have to do is write to Guideposts, 39 Seminary Hill Road, Carmel, New York 10512. When you subscribe, each month you can count on receiving exciting new evidence of God's presence, His guidance and His limitless love for all of us.

Guideposts is also available on the Internet by accessing our home page on the World Wide Web at www.guideposts.org. Send prayer requests to our Monday morning Prayer Fellowship. Read stories from recent issues of our magazines, *Guideposts, Angels on Earth, Clarity, Guideposts for Kids* and *Guideposts for Teens,* and follow our popular book of daily devotionals, *Daily Guideposts.* Excerpts from some of our best-selling books are also available.